American Government in Action

The FBI and
Law Enforcement Agencies
of the
United States

Michael Kronenwetter

Enslow Publishers, Inc.

44 Fadem Road   PO Box 38
Box 699   Aldershot
Springfield, NJ 07081 Hants GU12 6BP
USA   UK

Library of Congress Cataloging-in-Publication Data

Kronenwetter, Michael.
    The FBI and law enforcement agencies of the United States /
Michael Kronenwetter.
        p. cm.— (American government in action)
    Includes bibliographical references and index.
    Summary: Explores the diverse responsibilities and powers of
various law enforcement agencies in the United States, including
the FBI, the DEA, and the United States Marshals.
    ISBN 0-89490-746-8
    1. United States. Federal Bureau of Investigation—Juvenile
literature. 2. Law enforcement—United States—Juvenile literature.
[1. Law enforcement.] I. Title. II. Series.
HV8144.F43K76 1997
353.0074—dc20   96-30468
                                                     CIP
                                                      AC

Printed in the United States of America

10 9 8 7 6 5 4 3 2 1

Illustration Credits: Courtesy of the FBI, pp. 40, 41, 42, 43, 46,
51, 58, 59, 60, 63, 69; Photo by Michael Kronenwetter, p. 31;
Western History Collection, University of Oklahoma, pp. 22, 25.

Cover Illustration: Courtesy of the FBI

Contents

On the Job

September 1962. A young man arrives on the campus of the University of Mississippi to enroll for the fall semester. His name is James Meredith. In all eighty-four years of the university's existence, this has never happened before. James Meredith is, in the term usually used in polite society at the time, a "Negro."

As long as anyone can remember, schools in Mississippi—and throughout the South—have been racially segregated by law. Black children have been forced to go to different elementary and high schools than white children. Black men and women have been forbidden to attend white colleges and universities such as "Ole Miss."

But the federal courts have ordered that to change. The state laws establishing racial segregation violate the United States Constitution, say the courts. Segregation in public education is illegal, and "Ole Miss" is a state university. It, along with all the other public schools in the South, must be open to Negroes.

Few African Americans have dared to apply, however. They know that if they do, they are likely to be attacked, and perhaps even killed, by angry whites who want the state university to stay white. Angry whites are in the crowd that surrounds James Meredith now as he approaches the building where he is to register.

Meredith is badly outnumbered, but he is not alone. He is accompanied by a somewhat older white man in a suit and tie and hat. As the two of them arrive at the front of the building, their way is blocked by the stern-faced deputy governor of Mississippi. He is not alone either. He is flanked by an armed and uniformed force of the Mississippi state troopers.

The mob that surrounds Meredith and his companion are not the only ones who want to keep him from registering. The state's governor, Ross Barnett, has announced that he will never allow a Negro student to be admitted to "Ole Miss," no matter what the federal courts say. That is why the governor's deputy is here—to stand in Meredith's way.

What is happening is really a clash between the state of Mississippi and the government of the United States. Of all the southern states, none is more stubborn and more determined to stay segregated than Mississippi. The man with Meredith is a deputy United States marshal. His job is to enforce the laws of the United States and the decisions of the federal courts. That job includes enforcing the court's order to desegregate the University of Mississippi.

The badge that the marshal wears gives him the full power and authority of the United States government. With that authority behind him, he orders the deputy governor and his state troopers to step aside. Tension crackles in the air. Members of the crowd hurl racial insults. The grim troopers stand tense and alert, waiting for their orders. No one is sure what will happen next. Only James Meredith and the marshal appear to be calm. Yet they are not calm, only quietly determined.

Which side will win out? The power of the state of Mississippi or the power of the federal government? In the end the federal power is greater—even in Mississippi. The deputy governor backs down. He lets James Meredith and the marshal through. Even the state troopers step aside. The first African-American student in history is registered at the University of Mississippi.

▲   ▲   ▲   ▲

March 30, 1981. President Ronald Reagan emerges from a side entrance of the Hilton Hotel in Washington, D.C. He is accompanied by his press secretary James Brady and by other White House staffers. Also with the President are several Secret Service agents.

A crowd of eager on-lookers waiting on the

sidewalk murmurs with delight, as people catch their first glimpse of the President. Smiling broadly, the President begins striding toward the black presidential limousine waiting at the curb, only a few steps away. Reaching the car, he turns and lifts his left arm in a farewell salute to the crowd.

With no warning a young man named John Hinckley steps forward out of the crowd. He raises a small pistol in his hand. He opens fire. Six shots crack out in rapid succession.

Even before the six shots have been discharged, one of the Secret Service agents has stepped in front of the President to protect him. He is struck with a bullet in his stomach.

Press Secretary James Brady is also hit. One of the shots strikes his head, causing brain damage that will stay with him for the rest of his life.

The President, too, winces in pain. A ricocheting bullet has struck him in the chest. His legs fail him and he starts to collapse. Before he can drop to the sidewalk, another Secret Service agent has grabbed hold of him. In one motion the agent not only supports the President, but lowers him into the opened door of the limousine, while shielding him from further attack. Within seconds the limousine is speeding off, already on the way to the hospital where the President's life will be saved.

In the same few seconds other Secret Service agents and law officers have grabbed the would-be assassin. Unwilling to use their own guns because of the crowd, they have wrestled the armed man into custody without firing a shot. But they have paid a price.

Wounded and bleeding on the sidewalk are three victims of Hinckley's shooting. Among them is Tim McCarthy, the agent who was struck in the stomach with a bullet meant for the President.[1]

▲   ▲   ▲   ▲

August 1987. A man walks into a New York boutique called Italian Fashion, Inc. The store's owner, Tony Spavento, greets him in a friendly manner. An observer would notice nothing unusual about this event—an apparent customer and a store owner greeting each other. Yet things are not quite what they seem.

The newcomer is, in fact, a customer, as he appears to be, but he is not there to buy clothes. Tony Spavento is not just the owner of a small clothing store either. He is a criminal broker, a deal-maker, who brings together buyers and sellers of large amounts of illegal drugs.

The two men have met before. They both know that the customer is eager to buy a large quantity of heroin, and that Spavento has arranged for him to come to the store to meet two other men who have the heroin to sell.

The dealers, Michael Modica and Vincenzo Miceli, are quickly introduced to the customer, and the three men leave the store. They walk quickly to a car that the two dealers have brought with them. During the drive that follows, when they cannot be observed by others, the deal is done.

Before long the car comes to a stop and the customer gets out. He is now carrying a package containing a kilo (kilogram) of heroin. The dealers drive off with $195,000 in cash.

For the moment, at least, everyone is satisfied with the deal. The sellers, however, will not be satisfied for long. Nor will Tony Spavento.

For the customer is not, as they think, a fellow drug dealer. He is an FBI agent. The deal he has just made is an important link in an undercover investigation that will soon lead to the arrests—not only of Spavento, Modica, and Miceli—but two hundred other illegal drug suppliers as well.[2] That investigation will become famous as Pizza Connection II, and it will come up again in a later chapter of this book.

▲   ▲   ▲   ▲

The incidents described above are just three examples of the work done by the "Feds"—the federal agents who work for the many law enforcement agencies of the United States government. In this book, you will be introduced to the most important of these agencies, and to the endless war that they fight against crime in the United States.

A Nation of Laws

The Pecos River rises in the high mountains of New Mexico, and flows down through the desert in the southeast of the state to empty itself into the Rio Grande River in west Texas. In the days when everything west of the river was a wild frontier, a man named Roy Bean opened a saloon in Langtry, Texas. Proclaiming himself a judge, as well as a barkeeper, he hung up a sign: "The Only Law West of the Pecos."

Even by the standards of the 1880s, Roy Bean was a terrible judge. He was a ruthless man who dispensed the roughest kind of justice with a law book, a six-shooter, and a rope. Even law-abiding citizens longed for the day when ordinary judges and peace officers would arrive and establish real law and order in the region.

In the meantime, however, many people were secretly glad that Bean was there. Without him, they knew that desperadoes would run riot. Ordinary citizens would not be safe in their homes and businesses. Bandits and stagecoach robbers would control the roads. Hot-tempered toughs would kill at whim. Whatever else that was said about him, Bean struck fear into the hearts of such criminals. Even Judge Roy Bean was better than no law at all.

▶ Taking Law Enforcement for Granted

Today most Americans take the rule of law for granted. We know that certain acts are against the law. If we commit them, we are likely to be caught and punished. Because we take law enforcement for granted, we rarely consider what society would be like without it.

Without laws—and the criminal justice system that enforces them—modern society would be a nightmare. Evil people would be free to rob, beat, rape, and murder at will. The weak would be totally at the mercy of the strong; the honest at the mercy of the dishonest; the kind at the mercy of the ruthless.

Law enforcement agencies—and federal police agencies in particular—are often criticized. They may deserve much of that criticism. Without them, however, it would be impossible to live in modern society.

It is said that the United States is a nation of laws, not men. We are governed by laws that apply to, and protect, everyone. These laws do more than forbid us to commit crimes. They protect us as well—not only from the criminals among us, but from the unjust power of the government.

The most obvious job of the federal law enforcement agencies is to catch criminals and put them in jail. This is not their only job, however. It is not even their most important one. The most important job of federal law enforcement is to serve the people of the country by upholding the rule of law.

▶ Kinds of Laws

These are different kinds of laws. *Civil laws* involve dealings between private individuals and organizations. If someone violates this kind of law, they can be sued by an injured party.

Criminal laws, on the other hand, involve actions that do not just harm other individuals or organizations, but harm society itself. These include acts of violence and theft. If offenses such as these went unchecked and unpunished, society would break down. No one would be safe. Because of this, such acts are considered crimes against the whole social order. That is, crimes against everyone; or to put it still another way, crimes against the state. For the most part, this book is concerned with federal agencies that enforce criminal, not civil, laws.

Laws are established, and also enforced, by every level of government. *Local laws and ordinances* are established by cities and counties. They set rules for behavior within those specific communities. These are the laws that tell people where and when they can park their cars, for instance, and how fast they can drive on city streets.

State laws define most kinds of criminal conduct. The great majority of the laws against common crimes such as assault, burglary, rape, and murder are actually state laws.

In addition to forbidding such offenses, state laws set the punishments for them. This leads to differences in punishment among the states. A crime that earns a five-year sentence in one state may draw twenty years or more in another state. Some states have the death penalty for a variety of crimes. Others have no death penalty at all. Some states never parole criminals convicted of certain, especially serious, crimes. Other states hold out the possibility of parole for all prisoners.

Local and state laws, then, are passed by local and state governments. They set rules for activities within local and state borders. *Federal laws*, on the other hand, are passed by the Congress of the United States, and they set rules for the entire nation. They also set penalties for criminals convicted of federal crimes anywhere in the country.

▶ The Bill of Rights

All federal laws flow from the United States Constitution. This is the document that established the United States government, and the one on which all other federal (or national) laws are based. No law that conflicts with the United States Constitution can be legitimately passed or enforced by any level of government.

As far as law enforcement agencies are concerned, the most important section of the Constitution is the Bill of Rights, which is made up of the first ten amendments. This section sets out the basic rights of all Americans, including people suspected of committing crimes.

Unlike most laws, which are designed to prohibit certain acts, the Bill of Rights was designed to establish certain rights and powers. It commands all government officials—including law officers—to respect and protect those rights. That is something the likes of Judge Roy Bean never did, but it is a fundamental duty of today's law enforcement officials. Perhaps it is the most important of all the duties of federal law enforcement officials.

▶ The Federal Police Power

Police power is the authority to enforce laws. As originally written, the Constitution did not give the federal government any specific police powers. The nation's founders assumed that most crimes would be prosecuted at the state and local levels. Even so, they understood that the federal government needed some form of power to enforce its own laws. This was given by the Judiciary Act, passed in 1789 by the very first United States Congress to sit under the Constitution.

The federal government's police power is limited, and most criminal law enforcement is done by state and local law enforcement agencies. That is because it is the state and local governments that have jurisdiction over most criminal matters. The federal government, however, does have jurisdiction in three important areas.

The first area is the protection of the federal government's own interests. The government has the right, and the duty, to protect its officials and property from attack. This means that it has the duty to protect the nation's air, water, and other natural resources; to protect United States mail from theft or destruction; and to protect United States currency, bonds, and other financial papers from forgery or counterfeiting. By the same token, it protects those bank deposits and other valuables that are insured by the federal government.

The government also has the power to protect its own honor, by prosecuting federal officials who misuse their offices and outsiders who attempt to bribe or corrupt them. If the federal government could not punish such threats to its integrity as crimes, it could not operate.

The second main area of federal jurisdiction is interstate commerce, or the buying, selling, and transportation of goods and services from one state to another. If this trade could not be protected by the federal government, there would be no way to prevent or punish criminals who operated across state lines. Criminals from one state could prey on citizens of other states at will. Federal criminal laws in this area include laws against stealing or embezzling from interstate shipments of goods, and laws against transporting stolen goods or kidnap victims from one state to another.

The third big area of federal jurisdiction is the protection of the civil rights of United States citizens, including the rights of freedom of speech, press, assembly, and equal treatment under the law. It is a federal crime to violate anyone's civil rights.[1] These rights are guaranteed by the United States Constitution, and it is up to the federal government to protect them, especially when the states will not or cannot do so. This was the case, for example, when the southern states themselves were determined to violate the rights of African Americans by segregating the schools and other public facilities.

Despite the limits on the federal police power, there are more than forty-one hundred federal criminal laws currently in effect. Some were originally passed by Democratic Congresses, and some by Republican Congresses. Altogether, more than one hundred and forty federal agencies work in some way to enforce those laws and to prosecute the people who break them.[2]

There is not room in this book to discuss all of these agencies. Instead, this book concentrates on some of the largest and most active of these agencies. These include the United States Marshals Service, the Department of Justice, the Federal Bureau of Investigation (FBI), the United States Customs Service, the Secret Service, and the Drug Enforcement Administration (DEA).

The First Peace Officers

Federal law enforcement has a long history in the United States—almost as long as the history of the nation itself. From the very beginning in the 1770s, each of the thirteen original states had its own laws, just as the states do today. These laws were enforced by state and local law officers, and people suspected of violating them were tried in state courts. However, as soon as the federal government was established under the United States Constitution, Congress began to pass laws of its own as well.

Once the federal government had its own laws, it needed its own courts. These were established by the Judiciary Act of 1789, which set up a system of federal courts to try cases involving federal laws. At the same time Congress recognized that the federal government would need its own law officers to enforce the orders of those courts. It provided them in that same Judiciary Act by establishing the office of United States marshal.

President George Washington appointed the first thirteen federal marshals just as the Judiciary Act was going into effect. The original marshals were all men, as were all law enforcement officials at every level in those days. It would be a long time before anyone considered the possibility that a woman could be an effective peace officer.

The United States marshals, then, were the very first federal law enforcement officers. Over the next two centuries, many other federal law enforcement agencies would be established, from the FBI to the United States Capitol Police. Still, even today, it is the United States marshal who enjoys the title of the "Federal Government's Peace Officer."[1]

▶ The Marshals' Job

Each of the first marshals was assigned to one of the thirteen federal court districts. He had many duties, including helping the judges to run the day-to-day business of the court. More dramatically, the marshal had to deliver court papers and warrants, and to make arrests of federal court fugitives. Once prisoners were taken into custody, it was up to the marshal to hold and protect them until the court decided what to do with them.

It could be a lot of work. As far as the marshals were concerned, however, the more the better. They wanted more, not less work because, instead of getting a steady salary, they were paid fees for each task. The more jobs a marshal did, the more money he made.

When there was more work than a marshal could handle, he hired assistants—called deputies—to help him. Since the federal court districts covered entire states, most marshals had to hire several deputies in order to cover the wide expanses of their territory.

▶ A Sad Distinction

Among the original thirteen United States marshals appointed by President Washington was Robert Forsyth. In his mid-thirties when he became a marshal, Robert had come to America from Scotland many years before. He had fought valiantly in the American Revolution. His appointment as United States marshal for the District of Georgia was, at least partly, a reward for his distinguished military service.

Forsyth might have been both proud and happy to be picked as a United States marshal. It was not just an honor, but an opportunity. The new post would provide him with a tidy income as well as a position of some power in his state. On the other hand, the job of marshal would not be an easy or a safe one. It had a dangerous side to it, as the fate of Robert Forsyth would prove.

Sometime near the end of 1793 or the start of 1794, Marshal Forsyth was given court papers to serve on two brothers named William and Beverly

Allen. It was not a criminal matter, since the papers had to do with a civil suit. Even so, the brothers had made themselves scarce, and it took a while for Forsyth to locate them.

Hearing that the men were staying at a home in Augusta, Georgia, Forsyth took a couple of deputies along and went to serve the papers on January 11, 1794. The brothers were at the house where he had been told they were, gathered with a number of friends, when the law officers arrived. Marshal Forsyth asked the men to step outside, but they refused. Instead, they bolted. Dashing upstairs, they ducked into a room and locked the door behind them.

Determined to serve the papers, Forsyth and his deputies climbed the stairs after them. Just as determined not to be served, one of the men inside the room fired a pistol at the locked door. The ball slammed through the wood and into the head of Marshal Forsyth. It was a fatal shot.

By his death, Robert Forsyth earned a sad distinction for the United States Marshals Service. Marshal Forsyth was the first law enforcement officer of any kind known to be killed in the line of duty in the United States.[2] Unfortunately, he was only the first of many federal law officers who would be killed on the job.

▶ On the Frontier

The young country spread quickly across the continent, and the United States Marshals Service

On January 11, 1794, Robert Forsyth became the first of many federal law enforcement officers to be killed in the line of duty.

grew with it. One after another, huge chunks of land fell under the control of the young and growing United States. The Louisiana Territory, the Wisconsin Territory, the Dakota Territory, the New Mexico Territory—all the way from the Appalachian Mountains to the Pacific Ocean.

The job of enforcing the law in these huge, thinly settled regions fell first to the United States marshals. Strictly speaking, they were only responsible for enforcing federal laws. Federal laws were the only laws there were until a territorial legislature was formed and began to pass its own laws. If anyone was going to protect the citizens from bandits and trigger-happy gunslingers, it would have to be the United States marshal.

It was an enormous job. As the only lawmen in an entire territory, the marshal and his handpicked deputies were responsible for keeping the peace over an area of several thousand square miles!

Eventually, of course, the marshals would be joined by other peace officers. Once a territorial legislature was established, it usually hired its own marshals to enforce the territorial laws. Each county would have its own sheriff as well, and most towns of any size would have their own town marshals. Even then, however, the United States marshals usually remained the most important law officers in the territory. After all, they had the power of the federal government behind them.

Many United States marshals combined their federal job with an appointment as a city marshal, or county sheriff. Their most important position, however, was always that of United States marshal.

▶ Politics and Controversy

United States marshals were political officeholders as well as peace officers. Appointed by the President of the United States, they were usually members of the President's political party who had been recommended by powerful party officials.

An appointment as United States marshal was highly prized throughout the West for obvious reasons. The marshals tended to be important and powerful men. Scores of candidates would sometimes apply for a single post.

Like other political figures, marshals were often controversial figures. Supporters of their own party might admire them, while members of the opposition party regarded them as villains. Unfortunately, their political enemies were sometimes right.

Not everyone who got the job of United States marshal cared very much about the law that they were sworn to enforce. Some had been criminals themselves before switching to the opposite side of the law. Others would become criminals after serving as marshals. Still others took part in criminal activity even while they were in office.

Gratton Dalton became a United States marshal in 1887, following in the footsteps of his older brother Frank. Frank had been murdered in Fort Smith, Arkansas, trying to arrest traders smuggling whiskey to local Native Americans. Many white Americans on

His brothers formed a notorious outlaw gang, but Deputy United States Marshal Frank Dalton stood on the other side of the law. He was killed while attempting to make an arrest in 1887.

the frontier feared the Native Americans, and it was widely believed that alcohol had a particularly bad effect on the Native Americans and might encourage them to revolt. Largely for that reason, selling whiskey to Native Americans was forbidden.

A few years after becoming a marshal, however, Gratton joined two of his other brothers to start the notorious Dalton gang of outlaws. The Daltons and their companions went on a spree of train robberies that finally ended in 1892. At that time the gang was all but wiped out in a bloody attempt to rob two banks at once in Coffeyville, Kansas.

Some marshals were fine law enforcement officers who could be counted on to enforce the law sternly and impartially. Others, like Gratton Dalton, were criminals who openly violated the law. Still other marshals were harder to define. It could be hard to tell which side of the law some United States marshals and their deputies were really on. The same was true of many county sheriffs and town law officers as well.

There were few courts and judges on the frontier, and not many jails. The relatively small number of peace officers who patrolled the frontier regions often had to interpret the law for themselves, and decide which laws to enforce and how to enforce them. They did not always agree with each other about these questions, and they often found themselves at odds with other lawmen.

Take the case of the famous United States Deputy Marshal Virgil Earp of Tombstone, Arizona, and his even more famous brother Wyatt. The Earps are best known for their part in the famed "gunfight at the O.K. Corral," which took place in 1881.

There were two political factions in the Tombstone area, and the various lawmen in the vicinity tended to ally themselves with one side or the other. One faction was made up mostly of the cowboys and the cattlemen who employed them. The other faction was made up of prominent townspeople. John Behan, the sheriff of Cochise County where Tombstone was located, sided with the cowboy faction. The Earps sided with the townspeople.

In the notorious encounter at the O.K. Corral, Virgil and Wyatt, along with their brother Morgan and their friend Doc Holliday, fought with a gang of cowboys led by a cattle dealer named Ike Clanton. It was the most notorious gunfight in western history, but historians still argue over who were the good guys and who were the villains. Some claim that Virgil Earp was a dedicated lawman, and the Clanton bunch were rustlers. Others maintain that Earp was corrupt, and in league with crooked townspeople against a group of honest cattle traders.

Even the acting governor of the territory, John Gosper, could not sort out the matter. "I conferred with the sheriff," Gosper wrote to the United States secretary of state before the gunfight. "He represented to me that the Deputy United States Marshal . . . seemed unwilling to heartily cooperate with him in capturing and bringing to justice these out-laws. In conversation with the Deputy United States Marshal, Mr. Earp, I found precisely the same spirit of complaint against Mr. Behan and his deputies."[3] No wonder historians are confused, even today.

However controversial many of them were, the United States marshals played a vital role in the settling of the West. In the days before a territory achieved statehood, the marshals were often the main, and sometimes the only, law officers the citizens had to protect them. As late as the 1950s United States marshals continued to play the most important law enforcement role throughout much of rural Alaska, the United States' last territory on the continent.[4]

▶The United States Marshals Service Today

The frontier is gone. The time is long past when the United States marshal served as the lone peace officer, upholding law and order in a wilderness. But the marshals still have an important job to do. In fact, their job has expanded enormously over the two centuries since the United States Marshals Service was founded.

Just as in 1789, today's marshals are agents of the federal courts. In 1789, however, there were only thirteen United States marshals serving thirteen federal court districts. Today there are over twenty-five hundred United States marshals and deputies, working out of three hundred and fifty United States Marshal Service offices, and serving ninety-four federal judicial districts throughout the fifty states, Guam, the Virgin Islands, and Puerto Rico.[5]

Modern United States marshals perform a wide

variety of jobs, ranging from the most routine to the most exciting. Today's marshals continue to serve federal warrants—search and arrest orders from federal courts—just as Robert Forsyth did more than two hundred years ago. They also enforce other federal court orders, as they did in 1962 when a United States marshal made sure that James Meredith was safely enrolled at the University of Mississippi.

The marshals have a special responsibility to apprehend fugitives from federal warrants, and to transport and guard federal prisoners. In addition, it is the marshals who provide security for the federal courts and who protect the federal judges, witnesses, and defendants who appear there.

Although law enforcement is still the main job of the United States marshals, they have many other responsibilities as well. As always, they help with the day-to-day administration of the federal courts; and, when the federal courts order the assets of a criminal operation seized, it is the marshals who seize it.

Today's marshals also have some very special responsibilities that their predecessors never imagined. Since 1971 a United States Marshals Special Operations Group is assigned to keep order during riots and civil disturbances as well as major natural disasters. What's more, it is the marshals who have the awesome responsibility of providing security for the transportation of nuclear missiles.

Lawyers and Law Officers— The Department of Justice

The United States Marshals Service was made a part of a new federal department named the Department of Justice in 1870. In the years that have passed since this department was founded, it has become, in the words of its current head Attorney General Janet Reno, both "the finest law firm in the world, as well as the most outstanding law enforcement agency."[1]

The great purpose of the Justice Department is etched in stone above one of the doorways of the department's headquarters in Washington, D.C. "Justice is the great interest of man on Earth . . . wherever her temple stands, there is a foundation for social security, general happiness, and the improvement and progress of our race."[2]

More specifically, the Justice Department has the job of enforcing and prosecuting the laws of the United States. Agencies such as the United States Marshals, the Federal Bureau of Investigation (FBI), and the Drug Enforcement Administration (DEA) track and catch people who break those laws. Then the department's thousands of lawyers prosecute those criminals in courtrooms across the land.

▶ The Attorney General

The head of the Justice Department is the attorney general of the United States. She has been called "the

This inscription appears over an entrance way of the Department of Justice building, in Washington, D.C.

premier Federal law enforcement official,"—and, more informally, "the nation's top cop."[3]

The post of attorney general was actually established in 1789, nearly a century before the Justice Department was founded. The attorney general did not even start out as a law enforcement official. The early attorney generals were simply lawyers who worked for the United States government.

Until 1853, in fact, they did not even work exclusively for the government. They fattened their incomes by working for private clients at the same time. They had to. Although the attorney general was paid a small salary, he had no staff and no budget for running an office. He had to pay all expenses himself, and if he needed help, he had to hire his own assistants.

Despite all this, the attorney general was an important person from the very beginning. The first attorney general, Edmund Randolph, was an old friend and lawyer of President George Washington. The President asked his advice on many issues and even invited him to Cabinet meetings.

Attorney generals have had a seat in the Cabinet ever since, and many have been good friends and close advisors of Presidents. Robert Kennedy, who was appointed by President John Kennedy, was actually the President's brother.

▶ Growing with the Country

The size and duties of the federal government grew with the country. With its biggest client getting bigger all the time, the job of the attorney general expanded steadily. It was not until 1870, however, that the Justice Department was founded to give the attorney general the resources he needed to carry out the legal affairs of the United States government. (For more than two centuries, all the attorney generals were men. It was not until 1993 that Janet Reno became the first woman to become the nation's "top cop.")

At the same time, however, the attorney general and his new department were given a massive new responsibility. In addition to doing lawyerly chores, the department would have to enforce the nation's laws, investigate crimes, and bring criminals before the courts.

To help it carry out its duties, the Justice Department was given charge of the United States Marshals Service as well as the United States district attorneys—who represented the government in all regions of the country—and the other officers of the federal courts.

By 1895 the Justice Department had grown to 1,560 employees. A century later it had swelled to roughly 97,000 employees,[4] and its budget had grown to more than $10 billion.[5]

▶ Bureaus and Agencies

The Department of Justice is divided into many different divisions, bureaus, and agencies. Some of these help form new laws and regulations. Some advise other government agencies on legal matters.

Others defend the actions of those agencies in court. Still others enforce the laws of the United States, prosecuting the people and businesses who violate them.

The *Bureau of Justice Assistance*, for example, handles federal government grants to local and state law enforcement agencies; the *Bureau of Justice Statistics* collects statistics on crime and punishment around the country; the *National Institute of Justice* carries out research on criminal justice issues and tests new crime-fighting programs to see how well they work; the *Office of Juvenile Justice and Delinquency Prevention* works with the states to keep young people from getting involved with crime; the *Office for Victims of Crime* helps develop and fund programs to assist crime victims; and the *Office of Policy Development* designs and coordinates new federal criminal justice programs.

▶ The Civil Rights Division

Founded in 1957, the Civil Rights Division enforces federal laws and executive orders that forbid discrimination on the basis of sex, age, religion, ethnic background, disability, or skin color. The most important of these laws is the Civil Rights Act of 1964 that forbids segregation of public facilities as well as discrimination in hiring and education. Other laws forbid discrimination in housing and other aspects of life in America.

Most of the legal actions the Justice Department brings under the Civil Rights Act are civil cases. However, violating a person's civil rights can be a criminal offense as well. Specific federal criminal statutes forbid racial and sexual harassment and physical attacks; the mistreatment of migrants and other poor workers; and various kinds of misconduct by federal, state, and local officials.

Most of these crimes violate state laws as well, and they are usually prosecuted by local or state authorities. When those authorities either cannot or will not prosecute, however, it is up to the Criminal Section of the Civil Rights Division to look into the matter.

The Criminal Section gets around ten thousand civil rights complaints each year. It refers many of them to the FBI for investigation. Out of them all, however, the Civil Rights Division ends up prosecuting only about fifty to sixty cases each year.[6]

Although a relatively small number of federal civil rights cases are prosecuted each year, those that are often receive great national attention. The most famous recent case was the prosecution of Los Angeles police officers for the brutal beating of an African American named Rodney King. The beating, which was videotaped by a bystander, shocked most Americans when it was shown on national television. When prosecution under state laws failed to result in a conviction, the Criminal Section worked with the United States Attorney's office in Los Angeles to bring four of the officers to trial for violating King's civil rights. Two of the officers were acquitted, but the other two were convicted and sent to prison.

▶ The United States Attorneys

Ninety-three United States attorneys and over forty-one hundred assistant United States attorneys serve in United States attorney's offices throughout the United States, the Virgin Islands, Puerto Rico, Guam, and the Northern Marianas. These are the prosecutors who bring cases under federal criminal laws.

United States attorneys also play a key role in setting law enforcement policy for the federal government. Another of the most important roles of a United States attorney is to coordinate the efforts of federal, state, local, and even international law enforcement agencies.

At the local level, United States attorneys also help to direct federal criminal investigations, decide which cases will be brought to trial, and prosecute the cases in court when they are. They are often assisted by other federal agencies, including the FBI and the United States marshals who carry out much of the day-to-day police work involved in the investigations, such as serving warrants and making arrests.

▶ The Federal Bureau of Prisons

When criminals are found guilty of federal crimes, they are usually sent to one of the more than seventy federal correctional facilities run by the Federal Bureau of Prisons. These range from maximum security prisons, where the most dangerous convicts are kept, to minimum security institutions, where certain white-collar criminals and other low-risk inmates are housed.

Some federal prisoners work for Unicor—or Federal Prison Industries—a branch of the Prison Bureau that manufactures items for sale to the federal government. Prisoners are not forced to work for Unicor. Those who do are paid a small sum and receive valuable training and experience that may give them a head start at finding work when they get out of prison.

▶ INTERPOL-USNCB

Cooperation between United States and foreign police agencies is carried out mostly through the United States National Central Bureau of the International Criminal Police Organization—or INTERPOL-USNCB, for short.

This very special Justice Department agency combats international crime by tracking criminals who cross international borders. In addition, the bureau assists some twenty thousand local and state agencies within the United States to enlist the help of—or to share information with—foreign police forces.

▲　▲　▲　▲

Most of the Justice Department agencies discussed in this chapter are little known to the general public. In the next chapter, we will discuss the one Justice Department agency that is known to everyone—the most famous police agency in the entire world, the Federal Bureau of Investigation.

The G-Men

When most people think about federal law enforcement agencies, they think first of the FBI—and with good reason. The Federal Bureau of Investigation is the main police agency of the United States government.

▶ The Origins of the FBI

The FBI was born in 1908 as a small branch of the Justice Department called the Bureau of Investigation. As its name suggested, the bureau was charged with carrying out investigations for the Justice Department. It remained a relatively minor agency until 1933. By that time the social upheavals of Prohibition, followed by the economic chaos of the Great Depression, had caused crime to soar.

New emphasis was being put on law enforcement in the early 1930s, and the small Justice Department agency was reorganized and renamed the Division of Investigation. Two years later it was given still another name. This third name was a combination of the first two—the Federal Bureau of Investigation. This time the name stuck.

Under its ambitious director J. Edgar Hoover, the FBI soon established itself as the nation's best known law enforcement agency. In that decade a number of violent and colorful criminals were capturing the public's imagination. Ordinary citizens were half-thrilled, half-terrified to hear of their exploits. Mobsters such as George "Machine Gun" Kelly, and bank-robbing killers such as the young couple known as Bonnie and Clyde, were becoming famous throughout the country for their criminal exploits. The FBI became famous by fighting them.

The most triumphant moment in the early history of the FBI came on July 22, 1934, when federal agents surrounded the entrance to the Biograph movie theater in Chicago. At that time the head of a gang of bank robbers, John Dillinger, was one of the most notorious criminals and had twice been declared "Public Enemy #1" by the FBI.

Dillinger was a romantic figure to many Americans, thanks to his good looks, his raffish manner, and the audacious daring that marked his best known exploits. He was infamously slippery. Four months before he had escaped from prison by whittling a gun out of wood, coloring it with shoe polish, and using it to frighten the guards into letting him go. Twice since then he had fought his way out of tough situations, leaving dead policemen in his wake.

The Chicago office of the FBI, headed by Special Agent Melvin Purvis, had been tipped off that John Dillinger was inside the Biograph theater. The tip had come from a woman who was Dillinger's date that night and who was with him at the movie. When the couple came out of the theater, the FBI agents were

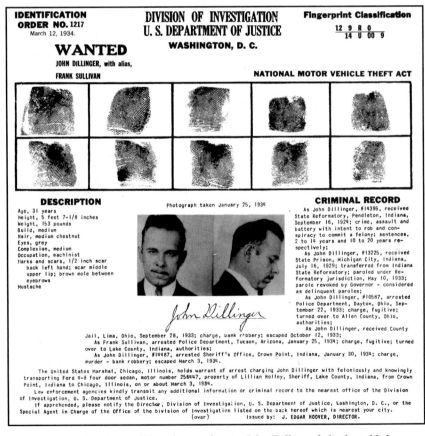

The gunning down of the infamous fugitive John Dillinger helped establish the FBI's reputation as the nation's premiere law enforcement agency.

waiting. Dillinger seemed to spot them and may have reached for a gun. The agents took no chances. They opened fire, and Dillinger fell dead on the sidewalk.

By the next day word had spread throughout the country. The "G-Men"—as the FBI men were becoming known—had ended the criminal career of Public Enemy #1. Later that same year FBI agents, led by

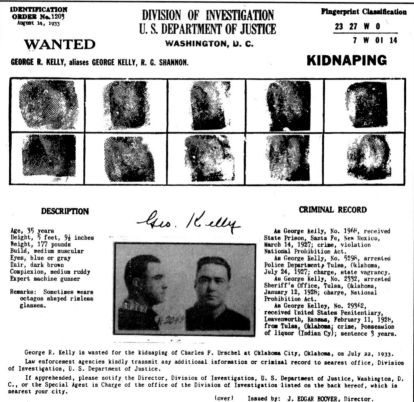

By August 1933, the Bureau of Investigation had been reorganized and renamed the Division of Investigation. This wanted notice for George R. Kelly noted that he was an "expert machine gunner." He would soon become known to the public as "Machine Gun" Kelly.

the same Melvin Purvis, gunned down the almost equally notorious killer "Pretty Boy" Floyd.

By the end of 1934 the FBI director could make a proud but bloody boast:

> John Dillinger, the flagbearer of lawlessness, is dead, killed by federal bullets. "Pretty Boy" Floyd, who for years laughed at the law, lies in his grave, dead of gunshot wounds inflicted in open battle by our special agents. The career of "Baby Face

IDENTIFICATION ORDER NO. 1227
May 21, 1934.

DIVISION OF INVESTIGATION
U. S. DEPARTMENT OF JUSTICE

WASHINGTON, D. C.

WANTED

MRS. ROY THORNTON, aliases BONNIE BARROW,

MRS. CLYDE BARROW, BONNIE PARKER.

NATIONAL MOTOR VEHICLE THEFT ACT

WANTED

CLYDE CHAMPION BARROW, aliases CLYDE BARROW, ROY BAILEY, JACK HALE, ELDIN WILLIAMS, ELVIN WILLIAMS.

DESCRIPTION

Age, 23 years (1933); Height, 5 feet, 5 inches; Weight, 100 pounds; Build, slender; Hair, auburn, bobbed; originally blonde; Eyes, blue; Complexion, fair; Scars and marks, bullet wound left foot next to little toe; bullet in left knee; burn scar on right leg from hip to knee; Peculiarities, walks with both knees slightly buckled.

RELATIVES:

Roy Thornton, husband, Texas
  State Penitentiary
Mrs. J. T. (Emma) Parker, mother, 1216
  South Lamar St., Dallas, Texas
Mrs. Billie Parker Mace, sister, 1216
  South Lamar St., Dallas, Texas
Hubert (Buster) Parker, brother,
  Gladewater, Texas
Nellie Gonzales, half-sister, Harwood,
  Gonzales County, Texas.

CRIMINAL RECORD

Arrested sheriff's office, Kaufman, Texas, June 16, 1932; charge, burglary; released.

DESCRIPTION

Age, 23 years; Height, 5 feet, 7 inches, bare feet; Weight, 150 pounds; Build, medium; Hair, dark brown, wavy; reported dyed black; Eyes, hazel; Complexion, light, Scars and marks, shield and anchor with "U.S.N." on right forearm, outer; girl's bust, left inner forearm; bullet wound through both legs just above knees.

RELATIVES:

Henry Barrow, father, Rural Route 6,
  Dallas, Texas
Mrs. Cumie Barrow, mother, Rural Route 6,
  Dallas, Texas
L. C. Barrow, brother, County Jail,
  Dallas, Texas
Marie Barrow, sister, Rural Route 6,
  Dallas, Texas
Mrs. Artie Winkler, sister, Sanger Hotel
  Apartments, Dallas, Texas
Mrs. Nellie Cowan, sister, Sanger Hotel
  Apartments, Dallas, Texas
Mrs. Jim Muckelroy, aunt, Martinsville, Texas
Mrs. Belle Briggs, aunt, Dallas, Texas
Frank Barrow, uncle, Eureka, Navarro County,
  Texas
Jim Barrow, uncle, Streetman, Texas
D. Brown, cousin, Martinsville, Texas
Bertha Graham, cousin, Tyler, Texas
Claud Linthicum, cousin, San Angelo, Texas
Rommie Linthicum, cousin, San Angelo, Texas.

CRIMINAL RECORD

Criminal record and fingerprints can be obtained from Identification Order No. 1211, issued October 24, 1933.

Clyde Champion Barrow and Bonnie Parker constantly travel together and extreme caution must be exercised by arresting officers as they are wanted in connection with assault and murder of officers.

Complaint was filed at Dallas, Texas, on May 20, 1933, charging Clyde Champion Barrow and Bonnie Parker with transporting Ford Coupe, Motor No. A-1878100, property of Dr. E. L. Damron of Effingham, Illinois, from Dallas, Texas, to Pawhuska, Oklahoma, on or about September 16, 1932.

Law enforcement agencies kindly transmit any additional information or criminal record to the nearest office of the Division of Investigation, U. S. Department of Justice.

If apprehended, please notify the Director, Division of Investigation, U. S. Department of Justice, Washington, D. C., or the Special Agent in Charge of the office of the Division of Investigation listed on the back hereof which is nearest your city.

(over)

Issued by: **J. EDGAR HOOVER, DIRECTOR.**

A Division of Investigation wanted notice for Mr. and Mrs. Clyde Barrow, the young couple better known to the public as the bank-robbing killers Bonnie and Clyde.

Nelson" is over; he died of seventeen bullet wounds while two of the finest men I ever knew gave their own clean lives that they might serve society by ending his filthy one. . . .That is progress.[1]

The G-Men of the FBI had established themselves as America's leading crimebusters.

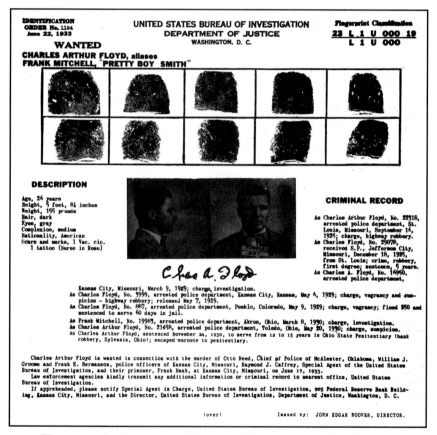

The agency that became the FBI was still known as the United States Bureau of Investigation when it issued this wanted notice for Charles Arthur Floyd, or "Pretty Boy Smith" in June 1933. By the time he was gunned down by FBI agents in Ohio in 1934, this vicious killer was best known as "Pretty Boy" Floyd.

▶ The Search for Public Support

"The most effective weapon against crime is cooperation—the support and understanding of the American people." This quote from J. Edgar Hoover is inscribed in bronze on a wall of the FBI headquarters in Washington, D.C., and it says something fundamental about the way the FBI has been run.

More than any other law enforcement agency, the FBI has lived by a belief in the importance of public relations. Almost from the beginning, it worked hard to enlist "public support and understanding," both for its fight against crime and for the bureau itself.

An important part of this effort was always the attempt to make sure that the bureau got good publicity in the media. As early as 1932 the bureau supplied information to a radio show putting on a drama about the FBI. That information helped insure that the program would show the bureau in a good light.

Two years later the bureau formed a whole division to handle its relations with the public and with Congress. Members of this division were not content to pass on information to the media. Some even went so far as to write their own stories about the work of FBI agents, and then get them printed in popular magazines.

Over the years the FBI has cooperated with a whole series of radio and television shows and movies based on FBI activities. Radio series such as *Gangbusters* and *G-Men* were given "inside information" on the FBI's efforts to track down such notorious criminals as the gangsters "Machine Gun" Kelly, "Baby Face" Nelson, John Dillinger, and Bonnie and Clyde.

There were two big reasons for the FBI's emphasis on public relations. One was to make people like and respect the FBI. This was important for building political support, and making sure that Congress would give the bureau the money and resources it needed. The second reason was indicated by Hoover's words on the FBI building's wall—to enlist the public's help in fighting crime.

Good publicity was especially important in the FBI's battle against the notorious bank robbers of the 1930s. Some of these vicious killers had become folk heroes. In an age when the banks that the killers robbed were regarded as the enemies of ordinary people, many Americans saw the criminals as dashing adventurers crusading against arrogant wealth and power. A myth grew around some of them that they were modern Robin Hoods, robbing from the rich and giving to the poor. This was particularly true in the Midwest and South, where the banks were hated for foreclosing on the mortgages of thousands of poor farmers.

Hoover realized that the FBI had to fight more than the criminals themselves. It had to fight their heroic images as well. Using popular stories, radio shows, and movies, the FBI created a heroic image of its own. In time many of the people who had come to sympathize and admire the criminals changed sides and began to root for the FBI instead.

Having learned the value of good publicity, Hoover and the FBI continued to foster it. Once television got popular, the FBI itself helped create a long-running series entitled *The FBI*. Hoover even published several books, including *Persons in Hiding* and *Masters of Deceit*, although he did not necessarily write them himself. *Masters of Deceit*, for example, was not written by Hoover, but by other members of the FBI.[2]

▶ The "10 Most Wanted"

Hoover cashed in on the good will that the bureau's publicity campaign created in 1940. That was the year that the FBI launched its "10 Most Wanted" list, publicizing the names and photographs of ten fugitives whom it was hunting.

In the 1930s, gangsters often opened fire on rivals from the rear of moving automobiles. Fighting fire with fire, special agents of the FBI received training in the same kind of shooting.

Citizens were requested to report any sightings or other information that they might have about the criminals' whereabouts to the FBI. The list caught the public's imagination. People felt involved in federal law enforcement, and tips poured in.

The original lists were so successful that the FBI has kept a "10 Most Wanted" list ever since. Posters featuring pictures of the fugitives have been common sights in post offices and other federal buildings for more than fifty-five years. Since the list was started, one out of every four of the criminals who have appeared on it have been captured with the help of tips from the public.[3]

▶ Fighting Subversion

The second great mission Hoover set for the FBI was fighting what he called the subversion of the American way of life by radical, or extreme, left-wing movements. Hoover was particularly hostile to Communists and Socialists because he feared that they would start a revolution in the United States.

The FBI is responsible for investigations that involve national security inside the United States, while the Central Intelligence Agency (CIA) is responsible for them abroad. Hoover believed that fighting left-wing American political movements was a vital part of the bureau's duty to protect national security.

Even before he came to the FBI, Hoover had led the Justice Department's so-called Palmer Raids. This was a massive arrest of Communists and suspected

Communists that took place on New Year's Day in 1920. More than six thousand Socialists, union organizers, and ordinary union activists were thrown in jail.[4] Some 556 foreign-born Communists were deported. Most of the rest were released.

As FBI director, Hoover would continue his campaign against Communists for the rest of his life. The FBI would keep files on everyone it suspected of radical political beliefs and sympathies with Socialist movements here or abroad.

During World War II (1939–1945), Hoover's FBI turned its attention primarily to uncovering enemy subversion and sabotage. The FBI was successful enough that German and Japanese efforts to penetrate United States government secrets and to sabotage United States war industries never did any serious damage to the United States war effort.

▶ The Rosenbergs and the "Red Hunts"

After the war Hoover turned the FBI's attentions back to fighting Communists, or Reds, as they were sometimes called. The FBI played a big role in the effort to expose Communist spies and sympathizers in the United States during the late 1940s and 1950s.

The bureau's greatest success came in 1950, when agents arrested an electrical engineer named Julius Rosenberg and his wife Ethel. The Rosenbergs were charged with conspiring with three other people to send secret information about the United States atomic bomb to the Soviet Union. They insisted that they were innocent, and many Americans believed them. Nonetheless, they were convicted in 1951, sentenced to die, and eventually, executed in the electric chair in 1953. Refusing to grant them mercy and cancel the executions, President Dwight Eisenhower declared that their treason had jeopardized "millions of innocent people all over the world."[5]

The FBI considered the Rosenbergs' conviction proof that the Communist threat was real, and that its efforts to uncover "Commies" were justified. The FBI cooperated willingly with politicians such as Richard Nixon and Senator Joe McCarthy, a Republican from Wisconsin, who gained notoriety in their ruthless campaigns to uncover "Commie sympathizers" in the government, universities, and even show business.

Many critics felt, and still feel, that Hoover's FBI went much too far in its efforts to combat Communists. There was never any real threat of revolution in the United States they say. And it seems wrong for a federal agency to investigate American citizens for their political beliefs.

Aside from the Rosenbergs, few other Communist spies were ever found and convicted. Yet hundreds of Americans were publicly denounced as Communists. Many lost their jobs. This seemed unfair to many Americans, because most of those people were not actually Communists, and even those who were had committed no crime. The critics called the "Red hunting" investigations "witch hunts," implying that they were being carried out in an atmosphere of hysteria and fear. They accused the FBI of persecuting people in an attempt to find enemies that did not even exist.

The same critics charged that the FBI used illegal methods in its eagerness to catch imaginary Communists. They claimed that the bureau was wire-tapping people's phones, opening people's mail, and even breaking into and secretly searching people's homes. They accused the bureau of becoming the kind of secret police force Americans denounced in Communist countries.

In 1975 a Senate committee led by Frank Church proved that the FBI had, in fact, frequently used illegal methods. What's more, it was still using them. The hearings led to new laws to prevent such practices in the future. Most importantly, they forbid the FBI to investigate people solely for their political beliefs.[6]

The bureau has accepted the new limitations willingly. It has eliminated the illegal practices and restored the reputation of the Intelligence Division, which works to combat espionage and subversion.

▶ J. Edgar Hoover

The legend of J. Edgar Hoover towers over the history of the FBI like a mountaintop. Although Hoover was not there when the FBI was born, he was put in charge of the Bureau of Investigation in 1924, and became FBI director in 1935. He remained in the position until his death in 1972.

Hoover was more than just another head of

The legendary J. Edgar Hoover

another government agency. He was the guiding spirit of the FBI. He controlled its growth and development, molded it, and dominated virtually every aspect of the bureau for almost half a century.

While many Americans regard Hoover as a hero, others have a very different opinion of him. Many claim that he was better at selling the *image* of the FBI than at making it an effective law enforcement agency. Civil rights advocates complained that, under Hoover, the FBI trampled on the rights of left-wing, or even merely liberal, Americans in its frantic efforts to uncover possible Communists.

Rumors swirled around Hoover in his later years, accusing him of various kinds of personal misbehavior and hypocrisy. More importantly, they accused him of misusing his enormous power as head of the FBI. It was said that he had his agents spy on virtually all the important public officials, creating secret files about their sex lives and other possible sources of scandal. It was rumored that fear that Hoover might make these files public was the only thing that kept several Presidents from removing him as head of the FBI.

There is no doubt that Hoover was extremely hostile to politicians he considered too liberal or who challenged his power in any way. He spread vicious rumors about a variety of prominent Americans, from the Republican governor of New York Nelson Rockefeller to the Democratic Kennedy family to Reverend Martin Luther King, Jr. So, while some people regard Hoover as one of the nation's greatest heroes, others regard him as one of its greatest villains—a man who used the FBI to serve his own ambitions and prejudices, rather than to enforce the laws of the United States.[7]

▶ Taking on Organized Crime

The FBI made its early reputation tracking down the likes of John Dillinger and "Machine Gun" Kelly. But even Al Capone was a little fish compared to the big organized crime organizations of today.

The biggest of all is the Mafia. This elaborate crime network, which began in Sicily in the nineteenth century, was brought to the United States by immigrants who came to this country many decades ago. They called the organization the *Cosa Nostra*, which means "our thing," in Italian. The *Cosa Nostra*'s influence was felt first in the Italian-American neighborhoods of the big cities, but it eventually extended its tentacles of crime across the country.

The Mafia was, and is, divided into separate but connected crime "families." Each family is headed by a different leader, known as a "boss," "don," or "godfather." These families made huge amounts of money by controlling such criminal activities as gambling, loan-sharking, prostitution, illegal drugs, extortion, and labor union racketeering.

Using some of its profits to buy legitimate businesses, and some to bribe political and police officials, the Mafia made itself into a powerful national and international crime organization.

For a long time the FBI shied away from

investigating the Mafia. FBI officials even suggested that there was no proof that such an organization even existed. Some critics said that Hoover did not want to take on the Mafia because he liked FBI investigations to lead to arrests and convictions. These were hard to get against high-level mob figures. The godfathers rarely committed murders or robberies themselves. They had lower-level mobsters to do their dirty work. Going after them would take too much of the FBI's resources, and offer too little hope of getting convictions in return.

Hoover may have had other reasons for shying away from the mob as well. Hoover's supporters explain his blindness toward organized crime by saying that he was worried about the integrity of his agents, and the precious reputation of the FBI. The Mafia was notorious for buying off police and public officials. Hoover did not want his agents tempted by the kind of money the Mafia could offer them. Hoover's critics suggest that he may have had some kind of association with organized crime figures himself.

Despite FBI efforts to ignore the Mafia's existence, evidence of the organization kept popping up before the public. In 1951 Senate hearings led by Senator Estes Kefauver of Tennessee reported that organized crime was a vast and growing industry in the United States. In November 1957, state police stumbled upon a meeting of important mob figures from several American cities—and some from abroad—in Appalachian, New York. It was clear that the Mafia did exist, and that it was a major problem.

Finally, Hoover and the FBI had no choice. There

was no way for the nation's leading crime fighting agency to avoid taking on the nation's biggest crime organization.

▶ RICO

In the years since J. Edgar Hoover, the FBI has been more successful in its battles against the Mafia than Hoover, or its critics, ever thought it would be. Partly this is because the effort to prosecute mobsters has been greatly aided by two unusual federal laws.

The first is the federal conspiracy statute, which makes it a crime for someone to "combine or conspire" with anyone else to commit a federal crime.[8]

The second—the Racketeer Influenced and Corrupt Organizations Act (RICO)—makes it a federal crime to use profits from a "pattern of racketeering" to buy or invest in any "enterprise" that takes part in interstate commerce.[9] RICO also adds to the punishment for being a mobster, by allowing United States marshals to take over the financial assets of people engaged in racketeering. A "pattern of racketeering" can involve almost any major criminal activity, from gambling to murder.

In effect, these laws make it possible to prosecute mobsters for being part of a mob, even when prosecutors cannot prove that they have committed other specific criminal acts themselves.

Using these, along with more traditional laws, the FBI and the United States attorneys have won convictions against some of the biggest of all Mafia bosses. Among them is the famous New York godfather John Gotti. Gotti had once gloried in the nickname "The Teflon Don," because criminal charges never stuck to him. But the FBI managed to strip him of his Teflon coating. Gotti was convicted of ordering the murder of Paul Castellano, a rival for leadership of the Gambino crime family, and sent to prison for life in 1992.

The Mafia is no longer the only major crime organization operating in the United States. It is not even the only one with strong international ties. Among the newer mobs are the Triads. These Asian-based gangs operate in the nation's Chinatowns in much the same way the Mafia used to operate in Italian-American neighborhoods. Other growing criminal enterprises include ultra-violent Colombian and Jamaican drug rings, who are much more ruthless and violent than even the Mafia ever thought of being.

The responsibility for fighting the mobs is now in the hands of the bureau's Organized Crime and Racketeering Section. This section sets the priorities for the federal government's fight against organized crime. Specific anti-mob operations are run by elite Strike Force Units located in the twenty-one federal districts most plagued by large-scale criminal organizations.[10]

Challenges and Controversies— The FBI Today

According to a Justice Department publication, the objectives of today's FBI are "to have a significant impact on criminal activity, to investigate civil matters in which the federal government has an interest, and to provide the executive branch with information relating to national security."[1]

The FBI is responsible for enforcing 271 different federal laws.[2] These crimes include several violent crimes, such as kidnapping and terrorism, as well as foreign espionage inside the United States, racketeering, the transportation of stolen goods across state lines, hate crimes, and certain kinds of racial discrimination.

The J. Edgar Hoover building, which houses the national headquarters of the FBI, covers a whole

The FBI Shield

city block on Pennsylvania Avenue, in Washington, D.C. In addition to offices and work space for more than nine hundred FBI agents and six thousand other employees, the building contains some of the most high-tech forensic laboratories in the world. The five hundred or so scientists, technicians, and other experts who work in these labs spend their time analyzing evidence of every kind: blood, hair, fibers, teeth, skin, body fluids, bullets, knives, firearms, metals and rocks, handwriting, papers, and inks—anything that could form part of a crime investigation.

The FBI's headquarters are located in the J. Edgar Hoover Building in Washington, D.C.

The FBI labs do not limit themselves to FBI investigations. They also analyze evidence for local and state authorities. When their test results are used by local prosecutors, FBI experts will often testify about their findings in the state criminal courts.

Even larger than the massive headquarters building in Washington, is the vast complex of twenty-one buildings known as the FBI Academy in Quantico, Virginia. This is where men and women are trained to become FBI agents. It is also where experienced agents—and thousands of other law officers from around the country—come to receive special training in new, sophisticated crime-fighting techniques.

The bureau has major field offices in fifty-six

The FBI Academy in Quantico, Virginia trains new agents and other law enforcement officers in modern crime fighting methods.

United States cities, and smaller offices in almost every city and town of any size in the country. It also keeps liaison offices in several foreign countries in order to cooperate with the law enforcement agencies there on criminal matters in which both nations are interested.

▶ Information

The heart of any investigation is information. Perhaps more than anything else, the FBI prides itself on the quality and the amount of the information it assembles. A Justice Department publication brags: "The ability of the FBI to collect, catalog, analyze, and retrieve information on criminal activity has made it a model for police agencies around the world."[3]

Not all FBI analysis of evidence is carried out by the laboratories. A very special kind of evidence analysis is done by the profilers who work at the FBI Academy in Quantico, Virginia. These experts, skilled in forensic psychology, take all the available information about a crime and examine it in the light of information about similar crimes that have been solved and the people who committed them. Putting it all together, they figure out what the person who committed the crime is probably like. The profiles they come up with can be of great help to police agencies searching for the criminals, even when those agencies have no suspects at all.

A special branch of the FBI, known as the Criminal Justice Information Service, acts as a clearing house for information about crimes, suspects, victims, and evidence. It provides information, not only to the many FBI offices around the country, but to local and state police agencies as well.

The amount of information gathered and stored by the FBI is mind-boggling. The FBI's file index has 75 million names, and grows by a million more every fourteen months.[4] The FBI is also home to the world's largest collection of fingerprints, almost 200 million of them. Many come from criminals or suspected criminals who have been arrested and fingerprinted by law enforcement agencies around the country. The rest come mostly from people applying for military, teaching, or other jobs that require fingerprinting as part of the application process.

Millions of identification numbers from cars, guns, and other objects that might be stolen, as well as millions more pieces of information about missing persons and unidentified victims and suspects are stored by the FBI as well.

▶ Agents and Special Agents

The FBI has almost ten thousand agents. About one in every ten of them works out of FBI headquarters in Washington, D.C. The rest are stationed around the country.[5]

Becoming an agent is not easy. In a typical year, somewhere between 90 percent and 95 percent of the thousands of men and women who apply for the job are rejected. All applicants must be highly intelligent and in good physical condition. In addition, they must have a good background, be able to pass a security check, and hold a four-year college degree.

Would-be FBI agents can apply as young as twenty-three and as old as thirty-seven. Most of those who are accepted are in the middle or older part of that age range, however. That is because the FBI wants men and women who have already gained years of experience working in a related field. That field does not have to be law enforcement. It might be business, or the military, or the law, or any one of many other specialties that the FBI needs in order to carry on its fight against crime.

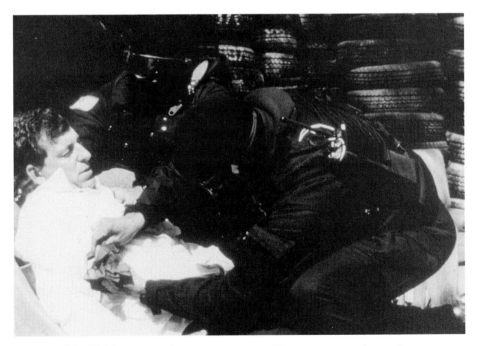

The FBI has its own hostage rescue team. Here, a team member receives training in caring for victims.

▶ The Tragedy at Ruby Ridge

The FBI has come in for some harsh criticism in recent years. Most of that criticism centers around events that took place at Ruby Ridge, Idaho, in August 1992. At that time, a combined force of United States marshals and FBI agents surrounded the isolated mountain cabin of a man named Randy Weaver. Weaver was a survivalist who had retired to a relatively isolated cabin in the Idaho mountains with his family to live as free from government interference as possible.

Weaver was reportedly heavily armed, and the FBI believed that he was engaged in some kind of illegal firearms activities. He had been ordered to appear in court to answer to firearms charges, but he had refused to go. He and his wife Vicki, along with their fourteen-year-old son Sam and an infant daughter, were holed up in a cabin set in a clearing in the woods.

The older Weavers were known to be bitterly opposed to the federal government in general, and to its gun control policies in particular. They were heavily armed, and the FBI considered them extremely dangerous. On August 21 a gun battle broke out, and both Sam Weaver and United States Marshal William Degan were killed. The next day Vicki Weaver was shot to death by an FBI agent while she was standing in a cabin doorway holding her baby.

Randy Weaver surrendered. He was later acquitted for his part in the gun battles, and most observers agreed that the FBI killings at Ruby Ridge should have been avoided. Faced with court action, the federal government agreed to pay Weaver millions of dollars in damages for what it had done to his family.

▶ Deadly Force

Three years later the Senate conducted hearings on the tragedy at Ruby Ridge. The hearings focused attention on the FBI's deadly force policies. Critics in the Senate attacked bureau officials for supposedly issuing an order that agents "could and should . . . shoot to kill" against an armed Randy Weaver after the deputy marshal was killed.[6]

According to the FBI agents who testified at the hearings, however, the traditional deadly force policy of the FBI was in effect at Ruby Ridge. Under that policy, "the decision to use or not use deadly force [was] entirely up to the individual" agent on the scene.[7]

This was the only reasonable policy, the agents argued. After all, it was the agent in the field whose life was at risk in dangerous operations. He or she was the only one who could judge how real the threat was and decide what action to take in response to it. What's more, he or she often had to make that decision in the midst of a confused, dangerous, and quickly changing situation.

Bowing to the criticism, however, the FBI eventually announced what it said was a new deadly force policy. In the future, a deputy attorney general explained, "Deadly force may not be used if an alternative reasonably appears to be sufficient to accomplish the law enforcement purpose."[8] What's more, it can only be used when there is a "reasonable" belief that there is an immediate threat to someone's life or safety.[9] The new policy applies not only to the FBI, but to all agencies of the Justice and Treasury departments.

Nonetheless, the killings at Ruby Ridge have severely damaged the FBI's treasured reputation. Many Americans are outraged at and deeply suspicious of the FBI and other federal agencies. These feelings are especially intense among those who share the antigovernment, survivalist views of the Weaver family.

▶ Domestic Terrorism

On April 19, 1995, a bomb exploded in a truck parked outside the Alfred P. Murrah Federal Building in downtown Oklahoma City. The tremendous blast tore off one whole side of the Murrah office building, collapsing the floors within. Several other buildings nearby were also damaged, and the tremor was felt thirty miles away.[10]

The date of the blast was the second anniversary of the Mount Carmel disaster near Waco, Texas. Evidence collected by the FBI suggested that the bomb was set, at least partly, to punish the federal government for that tragedy, and perhaps, for Ruby Ridge as well.

The Oklahoma City bombing was the most

deadly single act of domestic terrorism in United States history, but there have been many others. Terrorism is the use of force, or the threat of force, to frighten or intimidate people for a political purpose. It has been used by many groups over the years.

The anti-immigrant political party calling itself the Know-Nothings used violence to frighten foreign-born people in the mid-nineteenth century. In the 1930s workers who tried to organize into unions were attacked by "goons" hired by their employers. Some workers responded with terrorist tactics of their own.

After the Civil War, the Ku Klux Klan and other white supremacy groups used terror to keep the freed slaves in the South from claiming their rights. The KKK and other white groups continued well into the twentieth century to use fire and the rope to terror-ize African Americans, Jews, immigrants, Catholics, and others they disliked.

For the most part, local and state authorities were left to fight terrorist acts on their own. It was not until the 1960s that Congress passed laws making it a federal crime to violate people's civil rights by vio-lence or acts of terror. This allowed the federal government to prosecute people who prevented oth-ers from enjoying their constitutional liberties because of their victim's skin color, religion, or ethnic group. Since then, the FBI has played a major role in tracking and catching terrorists.

Among the terrorists or suspected terrorists caught with the help of the FBI were the white supremacists (some of them local law enforcement officials) who murdered three civil rights workers near Philadelphia, Mississippi, in 1964; the Middle Eastern extremists convicted of setting off the bomb that killed six people in the World Trade Center in New York City in 1993; and the two suspects charged with the Oklahoma City bombing in 1995.

The FBI was also involved in the search for the so-called "Unabomber." For years someone had been sending letter-bombs to scientists and computer experts around the country. Several of the recipients were killed or maimed when the bombs exploded as they opened them.

Although the FBI apparently believed that the Unabomber was most likely a male individual, it could not be sure that the bombs were not being sent by a group. In 1995, in any case, the Unabomber offered to stop sending the bombs if major newspapers published a manifesto attacking the influence of high technology. The newspapers did so, and the Unabomber did not strike again before a suspect, Theodore Kaczynski, was arrested in 1996 on a tip from family members. Although it had played little part in discovering Kaczynski, the FBI would play a significant role in analyzing evidence in the case.

Despite its efforts in these and other major cases, the FBI tries not to get involved in ordinary terrorist investigations. Most terrorist crimes involve local incidents such as a small group of Klansmen burning a cross on an immigrant's lawn or a gang of skinheads attacking African Americans who happen to come into their neighborhood.

Federal involvement in such cases should be

The current FBI director, Louis Freeh, was appointed by President Bill Clinton, and sworn in on September 1, 1993.

limited as much as possible, according to Attorney General Janet Reno. If a case can be handled by the local police, it should be, she believes. It is only when there are patterns of violence being carried out across state lines, or when federal employees or property are attacked, that the FBI should get involved.[11]

Even in such cases, the attorney general says, the FBI may limit itself to providing scientific expertise or investigatory advice to local officials. Only in exceptional cases should the FBI actually take charge of the investigation, as the agency did in Oklahoma City and in the Unabomber case. Oklahoma City was suitable for the FBI because of the incredible destruction, and because the target was a federal building. The Unabomber explosions were federal matters because the bombs had been delivered through the United States postal system.

▶ Computer Crime

One of the FBI's newest challenges is online computer crime, including crimes against children. Federal laws prohibit using computer systems to spread child pornography or to lure children into immoral and dangerous activities. "We are not going to permit exciting new technology to be misused to exploit and injure children," declared Attorney General Janet Reno.[12]

Proving its seriousness, the FBI conducted a massive raid on September 13, 1995. Agents in cities including Miami, Dallas, and New York raided the homes of 120 people suspected of involvement in online child pornography or of using online computer hookups to entice children into sex. Twelve suspects were immediately arrested.[13]

The two-year investigation, known as "Innocent Images," that led to the raid was conducted by a combination of the FBI and the Justice Department's Criminal Division. It involved an undercover operation in which agents posed as minors, and extensive investigations that used the same computer services as those of the suspects themselves.

Standing Guard— The Secret Service

The United States Secret Service was the first federal agency established to fight a specific crime. This key branch of the Treasury Department was founded in 1865 in the wake of the Civil War. At that time an epidemic of counterfeiting was flooding the country with phoney currency. People were losing faith in the value of the money that they received. The whole economy of the nation was being undermined.

The counterfeiters had to be stopped, and the Secret Service was founded to stop them. Within a few decades the new agency had done its job well enough to restore confidence in the United States currency. By the early twentieth century the United States dollar was the strongest currency in the world.

The Secret Service has been battling

counterfeiting and financial crimes involving United States government securities ever since. Protecting the nation's money supply is a tremendously important job, but it has been overshadowed by another Secret Service duty—protecting the President.

▶ To Protect the President

President Abraham Lincoln signed the order founding the United States Secret Service on April 14, 1865. That night he and his wife went to see the play *Our American Cousin* at Ford's Theatre. While they we were sitting in the presidential box enjoying the play, John Wilkes Booth snuck into the box and shot the President in the back of the head.

Lincoln was the first President to be assassinated, but he was not the last. Fifteen years later James Garfield was shot to death by a religious fanatic named Charles Guiteau. American Presidents had suddenly become popular targets for assassins. Even so, Congress was reluctant to create a force of presidential bodyguards. In other countries dictators surrounded themselves with an armed guard that enforced their personal power. Congress did not want that to happen here. Yet, with two Presidents killed in less than two decades, something had to be done.

Although they had no official authority to guard the President, Secret Service agents took on the job. They began to accompany the President to public appearances, keeping an eye on the crowd for hostile movements. At least one agent was there with the next President to be assassinated, William McKinley, when he was shot to death in 1901. Unfortunately for the President, the agent was standing on the wrong side of McKinley when the assassin fired without warning.[1]

Congress finally realized that informal protection was not enough, and it officially assigned the Secret Service to protect the President. Even then, however, Congress made the assignment temporary. If the President's bodyguards began to act too much like a private police force, Congress wanted to be able to call off the Secret Service.

It was only in 1950, after two Puerto Rican nationalists attempted to attack President Harry Truman, that the Secret Service was permanently assigned to protect the President.

▶When the Secret Service Fails— The Assassination of President Kennedy

It would be fifty-one years after the Secret Service began officially protecting Presidents before another President would be assassinated. That tragedy occurred as a presidential motorcade rolled through the streets of Dallas, Texas, on November 22, 1963. President John F. Kennedy was smiling, waving to the crowds that lined the streets from an open-top limousine.

Secret Service agents had wanted to walk alongside the President's car, but Kennedy did not want to appear in Dallas surrounded by bodyguards. He felt that it would give the people of Dallas the impression that he wanted to be protected from them. Instead, the agents had been exiled to the running boards of the specially built Secret Service follow-up car immediately behind the President's car. The agents were on alert, their eyes scanning the crowd for signs of trouble, but everything seemed peaceful. Then, suddenly, shots rang out from high above the street.

The car containing the President, his wife Jackie, and the governor of Texas speeded up. Within seconds it would be out of range of any assassin's bullet. Immediately realizing what was happening, Clint Hill, a Secret Serviceman assigned to protect the First Lady, leaped from the running board of the follow-up car. Sprinting, he caught up with the President's car just as it took off. Climbing over the back, Hill scrambled into the rear seat, throwing himself over the First Lady and the President alike, shielding them from any further bullets with his own body. It did no good. The President had been hit in the head and he was already dead.

Today the Secret Service would probably insist on walking beside Kennedy's car, whether he liked it or not. It is not likely, however, that this would have made any difference. Because Presidents need to appear in public, it is almost impossible to fully protect any President from an expert or determined assassin.

▶ New Resources, New Duties

The Secret Service agents acted quickly and bravely in Dallas, but they acted too late. They had not been thorough enough in checking out the buildings along the route the President's motorcade would travel. Killer Lee Harvey Oswald had been able to establish himself in a sixth-floor room of an almost empty building overlooking the route. And as a result, the President was dead.

Congress responded by granting a big increase in the size and resources of the Secret Service. In the years since Dallas, the budget of the Secret Service has soared from less than $20 million to over $540 million.[2] This allows the service to be much more thorough than it used to be.

At the same time, the service's mission has expanded. In addition to Presidents, Vice Presidents, and their families, the Secret Service now protects a variety of others. Their charges include several high government officials, the spouses and the young children of ex-Presidents, heads of foreign governments visiting the United States, and representatives of the United States traveling abroad on special missions for the government.

In 1968 President John F. Kennedy's brother, Senator Robert F. Kennedy, was assassinated while campaigning for the Democratic presidential nomination. In the wake of that tragedy, the Secret Service was given the job of protecting major presidential candidates, along with its other charges.

In addition to its plainclothes agents who investigate financial crimes and travel with public officials, the Secret Service also has uniformed divisions. Among other duties, they guard the White House, the buildings of the Treasury Department, and the homes of foreign missions in the United States.

Along with most other federal law enforcement agents, the majority of Secret Service agents are male. In 1991 only 120 of 1,900 special agents were women.[3] Regardless of their sex, these agents are trained for a very special kind of duty and sacrifice. A fundamental part of every agent's job description is the willingness to throw themselves in harm's way to protect the people in their care—just as Tim McCarthy did when he willingly took a bullet in his own stomach to keep it from reaching President Reagan.

▶ The Capitol Police

The Secret Service is not the only agency responsible for guarding United States government officials. Most government buildings and other properties in Washington, D.C.—along with the federal employees who work in them—are protected by an independent uniformed agency known as the Capitol Police.

The Capitol Police have what amounts to local police authority over the Capitol Hill area in which the bulk of Washington's federal buildings are located. Their jurisdiction extends throughout the eighty-block area surrounding the Capitol building, which houses the Senate and House of Representatives. After twenty blocks, however, their jurisdiction is shared with the Washington, D.C., Metropolitan Police.

The Money Police— The Department of the Treasury

The Secret Service is just one of several law enforcement agencies that belong to the Treasury Department. In fact, the Treasury is home to some of the most controversial of all the agencies that enforce the laws of the United States.

The treasury is one of the oldest departments of the United States government. In fact, an early form of the Treasury Department existed even before there *was* a federal government or a United States of America! The original Treasury Department was established by the Congress of the Confederation in 1781, before the American Revolution even ended. Today's Treasury Department was established in

1789, by the first Congress of the United States elected under the Constitution.

The Treasury Department has one of the most important jobs in the entire federal government—it prints and protects the government's money. The Treasury Department is the nation's bookkeeper. It collects taxes, pays out federal salaries and debts, and handles the financial dealings of the United States at home and abroad. Along with these jobs goes a massive law enforcement responsibility—the job of enforcing the tax and currency laws of the United States.

▶ The IRS

The United States income tax is the most important of the many taxes and fees imposed by the federal government. The system for collecting income taxes is called "voluntary compliance." This means that, although a portion of most worker's salaries are withheld to pay taxes, it is still up to taxpayers to figure what they owe and to see that the government gets the money. Much the same is true of businesses and corporations.

"Voluntary compliance" does not mean that people can pay however much tax they want or decide not to pay at all. It is illegal for anyone to refuse to pay taxes, or to hide or falsify income to avoid paying their full share. When people do, it is up to the Internal Revenue Service (IRS) to uncover the fraud, collect the tax, and bring the criminal to justice.

The IRS first grew out of the Civil War

(1861–1865). Fighting the war was expensive, and the government had to find a way to pay for it. In 1861 Congress made a start toward paying its war bills by levying the first income tax in United States history. That first income tax was set at 3 percent of incomes above $800 a year.[1] In 1862 Congress enacted the Internal Revenue Act, clamping duties on almost every possible good and service to pay for the growing cost of the war. The IRS was established at the same time to enforce the new act and collect the new taxes.

That first income tax, which had grown as high as 5 percent at one time, was dropped in 1872. Even so, other federal taxes remained, and the IRS was kept in place to collect them. The modern income tax was established in 1913, and collecting it has been the main job of the IRS ever since.

This is an enormous—and enormously important—job. The income tax is by far the federal government's largest source of income. In 1993 personal and business income taxes added up to a staggering $628 billion, more than half of the government's entire income.[2] The IRS estimates that only about 83 percent of Americans paid their full share of taxes in the early 1990s.[3] This means that over a hundred billion dollars are lost to the government each year through nonpayment of taxes.

Some of this money is lost through simple mistakes or misinterpretation of tax laws. Only a fraction is lost through criminal tax evasion, but even a small fraction of $100 billion is a huge amount of money.

▶ The Special Powers of the IRS

Because the money collected from the income tax is vital to the operations of the federal government, tax laws are enforced differently than other laws. The IRS is given special powers and protections that other law enforcement officials do not have.

When people are suspected of breaking other laws, the burden of proof is on the state. If the police suspect that someone has forged a signature on a contract, for instance, they must prove the signature was forged and that the accused person forged it. When it comes to tax laws, however, the burden of proof is on the citizen. When the IRS suspects that someone has failed to pay enough tax, the taxpayer has to prove that he or she has done nothing wrong.

Other law enforcement officials have to get a warrant from a judge before they can order a citizen to produce his or her private financial records. IRS officials, however, have the automatic right to see any records that might prove or disprove the information on an individual's tax return.

In some cases the IRS is not just an investigating agency, it is the judge and jury too. When the IRS determines that a citizen has not paid enough taxes, it orders him or her to pay, adds a penalty, and charges interest for the time since the taxes were due. If the citizen objects, the IRS can seize his or her property.

This does not mean that no one can take the IRS to court. That usually cannot happen, however, until after the IRS has already acted. What's more, most lawyers are reluctant to take on the IRS. They know that suits against the IRS are expensive to conduct and hard to win.

There has long been a $100,000 cap on the amount anyone suing the IRS can collect.[4] Anyone thinking about suing the IRS has to realize that it will probably cost more to sue the IRS than the taxpayer could possibly win.

▶ The "Revenuers"

The Treasury Department was founded to handle financial matters, but it was not long before it found itself battling criminals. The department's first law enforcement responsibility came in 1791 when it was given the job of collecting a new federal excise tax on liquor.[5]

Many liquor distillers did not want to pay the tax. In Pennsylvania they not only refused to pay, they took up weapons against the Treasury agents who tried to collect the tax. When the job proved too much for the relatively small federal agency, President George Washington called out military troops to put down what became known as "the Whiskey Rebellion."

The federal troops put an end to what amounted to an armed uprising by the liquor makers, but many individual "moonshiners" continued to evade the federal tax by operating in secret. Other people tried to smuggle in liquor from abroad, and sell it without paying any tax at all. During the two centuries that have passed since the Whiskey Rebellion, the Treasury has had the job of tracking down these lawbreakers, and either collecting the taxes from them or putting them out of business.

After 1862 that responsibility was handed over to the newly established Internal Revenue Service. The IRS agents who tracked down hidden stills in search of taxes became known to the hostile "moonshiners" as the "revenuers."

▶ Enforcing Prohibition

In 1919 the sale of alcohol was banned in the United States by the Eighteenth Amendment. The Treasury Department and the IRS found themselves facing the most important law enforcement challenge in the nation's history up to that time—enforcing Prohibition.

It was an impossible job. Millions of Americans continued to drink alcohol in spite of the law, and them seemed willing to pay almost anything to get it! Within a few years scores of new criminal organizations, called "gangs" or "mobs," were formed to supply the public's desire for alcohol.

Illegal stills sprang up all over the country. Some of the rotgut they turned out was so bad that it was said to make people go blind. Smugglers brought in high-quality foreign liquor from Canada. Bootleggers transported both kinds of alcohol to speakeasies and other illegal dealers in practically every city, town, and village in the United States.

Agents of the United States Treasury Department took on the mobsters and bootleggers wherever they could: from the streets of the nation's big cities to the remote reaches of the Canada-United States border. The "revenuers" led the fight against illegal alcohol, but they were not alone. Prohibition resulted in an increase in crime on every level, and every level of law enforcement was enlisted in the struggle to dam the flow of illegal whisky and beer that flooded America. Even the United States Coast Guard got into the act, patrolling the eighteen thousand miles of coastline for smuggling ships.

▶ The "Untouchables"

For the most part the efforts to enforce Prohibition were a failure. The federal government never really put the kind of money or effort into the battle against alcohol that was really needed to stem the flow of illegal booze.

Local and state officials in the big cities were even less committed to the battle against alcohol than the federal government. One big reason was corruption. Money flowed to the gangsters like beer from a tap, and they used lots of it to bribe politicans and police at every level. As a result the extent of corruption was worse than America had ever seen before.

Whole city police forces were paid off to look the other way when the trucks carrying bootleg whisky rolled into town. If a gangster was somehow arrested, the judge was frequently paid to set him free. Local and state political leaders were bribed to make sure that they did not appoint more honest police officials.

One great exception to the rule of corruption was the crack team of Treasury agents led by the legendary Elliot Ness. The gangsters called them the "untouchables" because they could not be bribed. Although badly underfinanced and understaffed, Ness and his agents played a long cat-and-mouse game with notorious mobsters such as "Scarface" Al Capone who dominated the bootlegging business in Chicago, and "Legs" Diamond who ran a major mob in New York.

The untouchables' finest moment came in 1931 when they caught the infamous Capone, the most notorious bootleg gangster of them all. Although Capone had undoubtedly committed scores of local and state crimes—including murder and robbery—it was the federal agents who ended his criminal career by putting him away for tax evasion.

But Ness and the other Treasury agents were fighting a losing battle. Too many people wanted to drink alcohol for Prohibition to succeed. The "great experiment," as it was called, was finally ended by the Twenty-First Amendment in 1933.

Alcohol is no longer forbidden in the United States, but it is still taxed and regulated. That job now falls to a relatively new agency of the Treasury Department, the Bureau of Alcohol, Tobacco and Firearms, shortened to the ATF. The regulation of alcohol is, however, only one of many ATF responsibilities.

▶ Gun Control

The very year after Prohibition was repealed, the Treasury Department got another big job to do. The National Firearms Act of 1934 taxed and regulated the sale of machine guns and sawed-off shotguns— the weapons of choice of the gangs that had been spawned during Prohibition.

Bootleggers and other hoodlums had been blasting away at each other with these weapons on the streets of many American cities for years, sometimes catching innocent bystanders in the crossfire. By limiting the sale of these weapons, Congress hoped to put an end to gang violence at the same time it put an end to Prohibition.

The job of controlling the sale of the controversial weapons was originally given to the IRS. Gun owners protested that limiting gun ownership was unconstitutional. In 1939, however, the United States Supreme Court ruled, in the case of *United States* v. *Miller* that the Second Amendment only protected the kinds of weapons that would be used by a state militia. That did not include sawed-off shotguns.[6]

Enforcing federal gun control regulations has been the duty of the Treasury Department ever since 1934. It no longer falls on the IRS, however. By the early 1970s it had become clear that the IRS had too much to do. Collecting taxes was one thing, fighting mobsters, gun smugglers, and other violent criminals was another. In 1972 the IRS's more policelike duties were split and given to the newly established ATF.

▶ The ATF's Job Today

Today's ATF has about four thousand employees.[7] In addition to its gun control duties, the ATF collects about $13 billion each year in federal taxes on alcohol and tobacco. The ATF has other duties as well, including enforcing the federal laws against arson, and tracking down violators of the Contraband Cigarette Act of 1978 and of the Career Criminal Act of 1984.[8]

By far the most difficult and controversial job the ATF has, however, is enforcing the federal laws that regulate the sale of guns and explosives. The most sweeping of these federal gun control laws is the so-called Brady Law, passed in 1993. Named after James Brady, the press secretary who was seriously wounded in the assassination attempt on President Reagan, the Brady Law attempts to limit the distribution of handguns. Handguns are targeted because they are the cause of roughly twenty-four thousand deaths each year, the great majority of which are murders, suicides, or other crimes.

Among other things, the Brady Law requires a five-day waiting period for the purchase of handguns. It also calls for a national computer network to check potential gun buyers for possible criminal records or serious mental problems.

Passed a year later, the Crime Bill of 1994 bans the sale of nineteen specific kinds of automatic weapons. These weapons are controlled because, in the view of the government, they are essentially military weapons that have no legitimate private use. The bill also prohibits selling or giving firearms to certain juveniles and adults under restraining orders from the courts.

Before these laws took effect, virtually all someone had to do to sell guns legally was fill out an application and pay a $30 license fee. By the early 1990s there were almost a quarter of a million gun dealers in the United States. About three out of four of them were not even retail store owners, but people who bought and sold guns in their own homes, or even out of their cars.[9] With a budget that allowed for only twenty-eight thousand ATF inspections a year, the agency could not even check to make sure that it was not licensing known criminals to supply weapons to other criminals.

Armed with the new laws, however, the ATF got more aggressive in cracking down on shady gun dealers. By the mid-1990s, its efforts had reduced the number of gun dealers by one hundred and fifty a day.[10] ATF officials are predicting that the number of dealers will soon drop to a more reasonable number. Even if the prediction comes true, however, there will still be twenty-five gun dealers for every employee of the ATF.

Guns are still easier to buy and sell in the United States—both legally and illegally—than in any other country. There are also more guns in private hands here than anywhere else. The best estimate is that Americans own more than 220 million guns, which amounts to almost one for every American.[11] The ATF does what it can, but it admits that it lacks the funds to really control the trade in this vast arsenal.

▶ Controversy

Probably no other federal agency has been as controversial as ATF in recent years. The ATF's efforts to regulate gun ownership were bound to arouse the hostility of the National Rifle Association (NRA), which represents gun owners and the gun industry. The NRA has a powerful political lobby and has led a long campaign to discredit the bureau.

Only ten years after the bureau's creation, the NRA won the support of President Ronald Reagan's administration, which made a serious effort to dismantle the ATF. Treasury officials appointed by Reagan suggested dividing the bureau's duties and handing them over to other agencies within the department. Alcohol and tobacco regulation would go to the United States Customs Service, while firearms and explosives would go to the Secret Service. Although the ATF survived this crisis, its staff was drastically reduced.[12]

▶ The Tragedy at Waco

Not all the ATF's troubles are caused by the NRA. The ATF has done some of the damage to itself. Many people have accused the agency of being arrogant and ATF agents of being "cowboys"—eager to act tough and to throw around their weight.

These charges came to a head in the wake of a

disaster at Mount Carmel near Waco, Texas, in 1993. Scores of members of an odd religious sect known as the Branch Davidians lived in a large building at Mount Carmel. They were followers of a fanatical leader named David Koresh.

The ATF and other Justice Department agencies knew that the Branch Davidians had stored up a large arsenal of illegal weapons. When a force of ATF agents stormed the building in an attempt to seize the weapons, however, a gun battle broke out and four federal agents were killed. Some Branch Davidians were shot as well, and Koresh himself was wounded.

The ATF put the building under siege. Weeks of negotiation followed while federal agents tried to talk Koresh into surrendering. During this time the agents had reason to believe that Koresh and other adults in the building were sexually, physically, and emotionally abusing the many children inside the compound.

When the negotiators failed to convince Koresh to come out, Attorney General Janet Reno and the Justice Department decided to act. On the morning of April 19 government tanks rolled up to the building and started smashing holes in the walls. The tanks were met with gunfire from inside, but they continued to assault the walls. Special nozzles, sticking out where the tanks' cannons would normally be, injected a kind of tear gas into the building. The ATF's intention, Attorney General Reno would later testify, was not to harm anyone. The tear gas was only meant to force the Branch

Davidians into leaving the building where they could be taken into custody.

However, something went terribly wrong. Fire broke out, and within an amazingly short time, the entire building had first burst into flames and then burned to the ground. A few of the residents escaped the flames, but eighty-two of them—including many children and David Koresh as well—never came out.

The government suggested that Koresh, whom they believed to be insane, had ordered the fires set. On the other hand, some surviving sect members accused the ATF of deliberately setting the fires in order to kill the Branch Davidians. It is possible that the fire was actually a terrible unforseen accident caused by the tanks knocking over a lantern or by gunfire from inside the Mount Carmel compound somehow igniting the tear gas. Whatever really caused the tragedy, the incident left a black mark on the record of federal law enforcement.

▶ The Customs Service

Income taxes and excise taxes are not the federal government's only sources of income. The government also collects money from the tariffs and other fees imposed on goods and services that come into the United States from abroad. The job of levying and collecting this money belongs to the United States Customs Service.

Established in 1789 as a part of the original Treasury Department, today's Customs Service oversees roughly three hundred customs posts located at every international port of entry into the United States, Puerto Rico, and the United States Virgin Islands. These include every airport that accepts international flights, every ocean port, and every land border station between the United States and its neighbors. In addition, the United States Customs Service maintains eight offices overseas.

For the most part the men and women who work for the Customs Service have routine jobs regulating international trade. They are the ones, for example, who greet tourists coming into the country and inspect their luggage. Other customs employees contact import-export businesses to let them know about changes in the laws regulating trade with other countries. Customs agents also have important law enforcement responsibilities. They are the federal officials assigned to catch smugglers and seize contraband. These duties give the Customs Service a key role in fighting illegal drugs—particularly cocaine that comes from South America and heroin that comes from Asia.

The Federal Government's War on Drugs

The city of New York never really sleeps, but at 4:00 A.M. it comes close. In most neighborhoods, at least, there is a pause between the activities of the night and the first stirrings of the day. The streets are all but deserted. The buildings are dark and quiet. Even police activities seem to slow to a halt.

However, at 4:00 A.M. on one particular morning in April 1988, a major federal anti-crime operation was in full swing. Unnoticed by the sleeping city residents, 260 FBI and DEA agents were fanning out in a great web over the city. Similar webs were spreading over other American cities and in certain cities in Italy as well.

The center of all these webs was a single room on the twenty-sixth floor of the Federal Building in downtown Manhattan. This room was the FBI command center for the operation that became known as Pizza Connection II. The first Pizza Connection raids, which took place in 1984, had closed the Sicilian Mafia's vast network of pizza parlors, which the mob had used to distribute heroin. Pizza Connection II was casting its nets even wider, targeting many aspects of the Mafia's drug operations in the United States.

Now agents sat anxiously at the desks that lined the room, taking phone calls from the agents in the field. They entered what they heard into a computer system, and the result appeared on big screens up on the wall of the room. The movements and locations of the field agents were being tracked on maps of the city. The numbers of arrests were chalked up for all to see.

Within an hour more than one hundred drug smugglers, dealers, and mob front men and women were awakened from sleep only to find themselves trapped in a real nightmare. Each of them had been identified and investigated beforehand by federal agents, some of them working undercover. Now they were quickly awakened, arrested, and taken to jail. By the time the raids were complete, over one hundred more had joined the original one hundred in custody.[1]

Both Pizza Connections I and II were successes. The first closed down the Mafia's heroin operations. The second put many high-ranking drug criminals in jail. And yet it was not long after Pizza Connection I before heroin was once again easily available on the streets of America's cities; and for every criminal arrested in Pizza Connection II, there were many others waiting to take their place.

▶ The Enemy—The Illegal Drug Industry

Combating illegal drugs is by far the biggest challenge facing American law enforcement today. The illegal drug industry is a big business in the United States— and a very profitable one. A large quantity of street drugs is relatively cheap to make and can be sold for huge amounts of money.

Just how big the illegal drug business is can be measured by the incredible sums people pay for its products. Americans spend over three times as much on illegal drugs as on legal drugs; more than they spend on sports, or movies, or other kinds of public entertainment; and more than they spend on automobiles.

Illegal drugs cost American society much more than the price of the drugs themselves. As long ago as 1983 the United States Department of Health and Human Services estimated that drug abuse cost society $59 billion a year. That estimate included such expenses as the health care needed to repair the damage done by illegal drugs, the crimes addicts commit to get the money to buy the drugs, and the cost of catching and imprisoning drug criminals.

And money is only one kind of cost. The most terrible price America pays for the illegal drug industry is measured in personal tragedy. Uncounted numbers of lives are lost or damaged by the abuse of drugs, and many more by the violent crime that accompanies the illegal drug trade.

▶ The DEA

The Drug Enforcement Administration (DEA) was founded in 1973 by combining three earlier anti-drug agencies of the Justice Department into one. At the same time, those members of the Customs Service who specialized in the fight against drug smuggling were also put under DEA control.[2]

The DEA is now the lead federal agency responsible for enforcing United States drug control laws. Among its other duties, it investigates major drug criminals, and handles assets seized from them. It manages a national intelligence system that gathers and stores information on narcotics and other illegal drugs. It coordinates the antidrug efforts of other federal agencies, and of state and local agencies as well; and it conducts research and training aimed at reducing the national and international traffic in illegal drugs.

The DEA operates worldwide, working closely with foreign governments and police agencies to combat the foreign drug manufacturers and smugglers who export their products to the United States.

In addition to its own activities, DEA helps organize and direct what has become known as the "War on Drugs." This is the term politicians use for the national effort to combat the illegal drug industry in the United States and abroad.

▶ Declaring War on Drugs

The so-called War on Drugs was first declared by President Richard Nixon in the early 1970s. It was declared a second time by President Ronald Reagan in 1986, and a third by President George Bush in 1989. Like the war on crime, in general it is still going on.

The War on Drugs is fought on many fronts. In fact, it is fought on *every* front. Local police departments fight it on the streets of the nation's cities, where crack and powder cocaine, heroin, LSD, ice, and every other kind of illegal drug is sold on a retail basis. The United States Customs Service fights it at the nation's borders, where most of the drugs used in the United States are smuggled into the country. The FBI fights it in special operations, such as Pizza Connection II, that combine the dangerous work of field agents with careful planning and organization from headquarters.

Even the Defense Department has become a part of the War on Drugs. Americans have always been reluctant to get the military involved in fighting domestic crime. The military's job is to defend the country from foreign threats, not to police American citizens. Supporters of military involvement in fighting drugs point out, however, that the threat from illegal drugs is, to some degree anyway, a foreign threat. Most illegal drugs—including cocaine and heroin—are smuggled into the country from abroad. Why not use the military, with its vast resources, to help protect people from these imported dangers?

In 1984 ships of the United States Navy and Coast Guard temporarily blockaded the coast of the nation of Colombia. Operation Hat Trick, as it was called, prevented large quantities of Colombian marijuana from being shipped to the United States. Five years later, in 1989, the Department of Defense was given the authority to coordinate surveillance of ships and planes suspected of carrying illegal drugs to the United States.[3]

Inside the country, state and local authorities can call on the military for help in training their own police to conduct the War on Drugs. Under some circumstances, they can even request the use of special military equipment, including tanks, for use in anti-drug operations.

Even with all the federal involvement, state and local law enforcement agencies remain the real foot soldiers in the War on Drugs. In 1990, for example, they made over 1.1 million drug arrests, compared to only about twenty-two thousand by the DEA.[4]

▶ The Expense of the Drug War

The War on Drugs is expensive to fight. In 1991, for example, the federal government spent $10.8 billion attempting to control illegal drugs. More than $7 billion of that money was spent on law enforcement efforts. The rest went mostly to drug abuse prevention and treatment. Over $5 billion more was spent by local and state governments in the same efforts.

The United States Department of Justice alone

devoted $3.8 billion to the drug war in 1991—almost exactly one-half of the department's entire budget.

In a typical year the DEA will spend its entire budget on fighting drugs. The United States Marshals Service will spend 70 percent of its own budget on drugs; the Bureau of Prisons, 60 percent; the United States Customs Service, over 46 percent; the Bureau of Alcohol, Tobacco and Firearms, 42 percent; the United States Attorneys, 31 percent; INTERPOL, 25 percent; the Coast Guard, 21 percent; and the FBI, 15 percent. Even the Secret Service devotes 13 percent of its annual budget to fighting drugs and the IRS spends just over 2 percent.[5]

In addition to all this money, tens of millions of dollars are sent to foreign governments each year to help control the illegal drug traffic in their countries. This is done not so much to help them, but to keep the drugs originating in those countries from finding their way here. The majority of that money goes to Latin America.

▶ Wars That Can Never Be Won

Judged by the numbers of arrests, convictions, and imprisonments, the federal government's War on Drugs has been tremendously successful. Roughly eight out of ten defendants charged with drug trafficking are convicted, and the great majority of those are sent to prison.[6] Over 50 percent of all the inmates in federal prisons today are there for some drug offense.[7]

Clearly, law enforcement has won many victories in the War on Drugs. And yet the war has not been won. The same can be said of the federal government's war against crime in general. Neither war has been won. Worse, neither war will ever be won.

This is not the fault of the law enforcement agencies that fight these "wars." The very best law enforcement in the world can only discourage criminals. It cannot get rid of crime.

The causes of crime go deep into the makeup of society and of human nature itself. All sorts of personal factors work to turn some people into criminals and others into law-abiding citizens. All sorts of social and economic factors cause the crime rates to go up and down.

There is little that law enforcement agencies can do about any of these factors. They can only work as hard as they are able, with the resources they are given, to make crime as difficult to get away with as possible.

Many of the federal crime-fighting agencies discussed in this book do their jobs very well. They put more criminals in jail than the comparable agencies of any other country in the world. And yet crime continues to plague the nation.

"Law enforcement," Attorney General Janet Reno has said, "Is the most difficult job there is."[8] Perhaps this is what she meant. No matter how hard law officers work—or how well they work—they will never win the ultimate victory. The war against crime will always go on.

Glossary

attorney general, United States—The nation's "premier law enforcement official" and head of the Department of Justice.

contraband—Illegal goods being brought into or out of a country.

correctional facility—A prison or other place in which convicted criminals are kept.

criminal—Having to do with serious crimes against society.

duty—A fee or tax levied on products coming into the country from abroad.

espionage—Spying.

excise tax—A fee imposed on specific products or required to obtain certain licenses.

executive order—An order, signed by the President of the United States, directing the federal government to do or not to do something.

extortion—Gaining money through intimidation and threats of violence.

federal—Having to do with the national, or central, government.

forensic—Having to do with criminal investigations or legal proceedings.

income tax, United States—A tax imposed on the income of individuals and businesses. Laws requiring the payment of federal income taxes are enforced primarily by the Internal Revenue Service.

judicial—Having to do with courts or judges.

jurisdiction—A legal term meaning the right to exercise authority over a specific area. Federal law enforcement agencies have jurisdiction to enforce federal laws.

levy—To assess, or impose, a tax or duty.

narcotics—A category of drugs.

parole—The early release of a prisoner, under certain conditions, before his or her sentence is up.

Prohibition—The period between 1919 and 1933 during which the sale of alcoholic drinks was forbidden in the United States.

statute—A law.

subversion—Overthrowing, or undermining, a society or government.

surveillance—Following, observing, or keeping track of a person or thing, especially of someone suspected of criminal activity.

survivalists—People who fear that either nuclear war or violence among the races will one day make American society unlivable, so they prepare themselves to live without relying on the government or other social institutions.

treason—Betrayal of one's country.

warrant—An order of a court calling for the arrest of an individual or authorizing the search or seizure of property.

Chapter Notes

Chapter 1

1. Russell Miller, "On Guard for Bill Clinton," *Reader's Digest* (Canada), May 1993, p. 37. Reprinted from *The Sunday Times Magazine*, London, December 13, 1992.

2. "Inside America's Biggest Drug Bust," *U.S. News & World Report*, April 11, 1988, pp. 25–28.

Chapter 2

1. The three areas of federal jurisdiction are spelled out in more detail in Thomas J. Gardner and Victor Manian's *Criminal Law: Principles, Cases and Readings*, 2nd Edition (St. Paul: West, 1980), pp. 198–201.

2. United States Office of the Vice President, *From Red Tape to Results: Creating a Government That Works Better & Costs Less*, Report of the Task Force on National Performance Review (Washington, D.C.: United States Government Printing Office, September 7, 1993), p. 102.

Chapter 3

1. *United States Department of Justice Legal Activities 1994–1995; The Department of Justice . . . The Nation's Litigator* (Washington, D.C.: Office of Attorney Personnel Management, 1994), p. 103.

2. Glenn Gamber and Connie Clark, *To Serve and Protect* (Paducah, Ky.: Turner Publishing, 1995), p. 15.

3. Paul Trachtman, *The Gunfighters* (Alexandria, Va.: Time-Life Books, 1977), p. 25.

4. Frederick S. Calhoun, *The Lawmen: United States Marshals and Their Deputies, 1789–1989* (New York: Penguin, 1991), p. 150.

5. James D. Stinchcomb, *Opportunities in Law Enforcement and Criminal Justice Careers* (Lincolnwood, Ill.: VGM Career Horizons, 1990), p. 61.

Chapter 4

1. *United States Department of Justice Legal Activities 1994–1995; The Department of Justice . . . The Nation's Litigator* (Washington, D.C.: Office of Attorney Personnel Management, 1994), p. iii.

2. Punctuation added.

3. *Legal Activities*, p. 2.

4. Ibid., p. 27.

5. *The World Almanac and Book of Facts 1995* (Mahwah, N.J.: Funk & Wagnalls, 1994), p. 107.

6. Ibid., p. 49.

Chapter 5

1. Quoted by Nathan Douhit, "August Vollmer, Berkeley's First Chief of Police, and the Emergence of Police Professionalism," *Police, Prison, and Punishment, Major Historical Interpretations*, Kermit L. Hall, editor (New York: Garland Publishing, 1987), p. 330.

2. Ronald Kessler, *The FBI* (New York: Pocket Star Books, 1993), p. 363.

3. FBI official appearing on CNN News Reports, July 22, 1995.

4. Richard N. Current, T. Harry Williams, and Frank Freidel, *American History: A Survey*, Fourth Edition (New York: Knopf, 1975), p. 634.

5. *Chronicle of the 20th Century* (Mount Kisco, N.Y.: Chronicle, 1987), p. 736.

6. Kessler, p. 4.

7. For this view of Hoover, see Richard Gid Powers's *The Secrecy and the Power: The Life of J. Edgar Hoover* (London: Free Press, 1986).

8. Federal statute, 18 United States C.A. 371.

9. Chapter 96, Title 18, United States Code, 18 United States C.A. 1960 and 1961.

10. *United States Department of Justice Legal Activities 1994–1995; The Department of Justice . . . The Nation's Litigator* (Washington, D.C.: Office of Attorney Personnel Management, 1994), p. 58.

Chapter 6

1. *United States Department of Justice Legal Activities 1994–1995; The Department of Justice . . . The Nation's Litigator* (Washington, D.C.: Office of Attorney Personnel Management, 1994), p. 97.

2. Ronald Kessler, *The FBI* (New York: Pocket Star Books, 1993), p. 46.

3. *Legal Activities*, p. 97.

4. Kessler, p. 301.

5. Ibid., p. 350.

6. Marcy Gordon, "Use of Deadly Force Limited," *Wausau* (Wisconsin) *Daily Herald*, October 18, 1995.

7. Testimony of Dale Monroe before the Senate Judiciary Committee Hearing into the Ruby Ridge incident, September 14, 1995.

8. Sam Vincent Meddis, "Deadly Force Rules Echo Longstanding FBI Policy," *USA Today*, October 19, 1995.

9. Gordon, p. 00.

10. Nancy Gibbs, "The Blood of Innocents," *Time*, May 1, 1995, p. 59.

11. Attorney General Janet Reno, Justice Department press conference, Washington, D.C., April 27, 1995.

12. Laura Myers, "120 Homes Searched, 12 Arrested as FBI Attacks Online Porn," *Wisconsin State Journal*, September 14, 1995.

13. Ibid.

Chapter 7

1. *Inside the Secret Service* (Secret Service Productions, 1994), television documentary shown on *Discovery Sunday*.

2. Russell Miller, "On Guard for Bill Clinton," *Reader's Digest* (Canada), May 1993, p. 36. Reprinted from *The Sunday Times Magazine*, London, December 13, 1992; and *United States Budget, Fiscal Year 1996*, estimated 1996 Secret Service outlays.

3. Lois Smith Brady, "Secret Agent Women," *Mademoiselle*, September 1991, p. 228.

Chapter 8

1. Richard N. Current, T. Harry Williams, and Frank Freidel, *American History: A Survey* (New York: Knopf, 1975), p. 385.

2. Department of the Treasury, Internal Revenue Service, *1040 Forms and Instructions*, 1994 back page.3. Phone interview with IRS Criminal Investigation Division representative, Milwaukee office of the IRS, September 13, 1995.

4. Dave Skidmore, "Bill Would Raise Limit on Lawsuits Against IRS to $1 Million," *Wisconsin State Journal*, September 13, 1995.

5. Suzanne Cavanagh and David Teasley, *Federal Law Enforcement Reorganization: A Brief Overview*, A CRS Report for Congress (Washington, D.C.: Congressional Research Service of the Library of Congress, November 1, 1993), p. 3.

6. *United States* v. *Miller,* 307 United States 174 (1939).

7. Erik Larson, "ATF Under Siege," *Time*, July 24, 1995, p. 25.

8. Cavanagh and Teasley, p. 3.

9. Gordon Witkin, "ATF: Agency Under the Gun," *U.S. News & World Report*. October 4, 1993, p. 73.

10. Larson, p. 25.

11. Daniel Voll, "The Right to Bear Sorrow," *Esquire*, March 1995, p. 76.

12. Larson, p. 25.

Chapter 9

1. "Inside America's Biggest Drug Bust," *U.S. News & World Report*, April 11, 1988, pp. 19–20.

2. *Drugs, Crime, and the Justice System: A National Report from the Bureau of Justice Statistics,* December 1992, NCJ-133652 (Washington, D.C.: Government Printing Office, 1992), p. 84.

3. Ibid., p. 86.

4. Ibid., p. 76.

5. The figures on drug war expenditures in the above paragraphs come from *National Drug Control Strategy: Budget Summary* (Washington, D.C.: The White House, January 1992).

6. Computed from *Bureau of Justice Statistics, Compendium of Federal Justice Statistics, 1989*, NCJ-134730, May 1992.

7. *Drugs, Crime, and the Justice System*, p. 195.

8. Testimony before the Joint (United States House and Senate) Subcommittee on Waco, August 1, 1995.

Further Reading

Calder, James D. *The Origins and Development of Federal Crime Control Policy: Herbert Hoover's Initiatives.* Westport, Conn.: Praeger Publishers, 1993.

Drugs, Crime, and the Justice System: A National Report from the Bureau of Justice Statistics (December 1992, NCJ-133652). Washington, D.C.: Government Printing Office, 1992.

FBI Facts and History. Washington, D.C.: United States Department of Justice, 1992.

Kessler, Ronald. *The FBI.* New York: Pocket Books, 1993.

Kronenwetter, Michael. *Drugs in America: The Users, The Suppliers, The War on Drugs.* Englewood Cliffs, N.J.: Julian Messner, 1990.

Pistone, Joseph D. *Donnie Brasco: My Life in the Mafia.* New York: Signet, 1987.

Powers, Richard Gid. *The Secrecy and the Power: The Life of J. Edgar Hoover.* London: Free Press, 1986.

Torres, Donald A. *A Handbook of Federal Police and Investigative Agencies.* Westport, Conn.: Greenwood Press, 1985.

Turner, William W. *Hoover's FBI: The Men and the Myth.* Sherbourne Press, 1970.

United States Department of Justice Legal Activities 1994–1995; The Department of Justice . . . The Nation's Litigator. Washington, D.C.: Office of Attorney Personnel Management, 1994.

U.S. Customs Service: Protectors of Independence Since 1789. Washington, D.C.: Department of the Treasury, U.S. Customs Service, 1989.

Index